AIR TRAVEL'S BARGAIN BASEMENT

The International Directory of Consolidators, Bucket Shops, and Other Sources of Discount Travel

by

Kelly Monaghan

Air Travel's
Bargain Basement

✈ ✈ ✈

Published by:
The Intrepid Traveler
Post Office Box 438
New York, NY 10034, USA
http://www.intrepidtraveler.com

Copyright © 2000 by Kelly Monaghan
First Edition
Printed in Canada
Book Jacket: George Foster, Foster & Foster, Inc.

Library of Congress Catalog Card Number: 99-71538

ISBN: 1-887140-13-1

Please Note

Although the author and the publisher have made every effort to ensure the completeness and accuracy of this guide, we assume no responsibility for omissions, inaccuracies, errors, or inconsistencies that may appear. Any slights of people or organizations are unintentional.

It must be understood that the listings in this guide in no way constitute an endorsement or guarantee on the part of the author or publisher. All readers who deal with the consolidators and other companies listed herein do so at their own risk.

This book is sold with the understanding that neither the author nor the publisher are engaged in rendering legal or other professional advice. If legal or other expert assistance is required, the reader should consult with a competent professional.

The author and The Intrepid Traveler shall have neither liability nor responsibility to any person or entity with respect to any loss or damage caused, or alleged to be caused, directly or indirectly, by the information contained herein.

Also by Kelly Monaghan

Fly Cheap!

Air Courier Bargains:
How To Travel World-Wide For
Next To Nothing

Orlando's OTHER Theme Parks:
What To Do When You've Done Disney

Home-Based Travel Agent:
How To Cash In On The Exciting
NEW World Of Travel Marketing

The Intrepid Traveler's Complete Desk Reference
(co-author)

A Shopper's Guide To Independent Agent Opportunities

Table of Contents

Chapter One

Introduction

Let's say you have to be in Milan next week to seal a big business deal. Your excitement is equalled only by your horror at the exorbitant "unrestricted" coach ticket you are going to be forced to buy — after all, it's too late to qualify for those super-saver fares. Before you say, "There go the profits," reach for the phone and call Moment's Notice. They'll give you a fare at or close to the super-saver fare the airline says you can't have.

Or perhaps you're planning a vacation overseas for you and your spouse. You want to go some place different, a bit off the beaten path. You check your copy of my book, *Air Courier Bargains,* and find there's just nothing for Transylvania. Do you forget about it? No, you pick up the phone and call Adventure International Travel Service in Lakewood, Ohio, one of the growing number of consolidators specializing in travel to low-cost Eastern European destinations where the dollar still commands some respect; you get the lowest fare possible.

Perhaps you are looking for a super-cheap domestic ticket. In that case, check out Mr. Cheap's Travel at one of its two locations. They'll be able to get you up to 20 percent off on a major American airline whose name, for legal purposes, must be shrouded in mystery.

Or let's say you simply want to squeeze a little extra money out of the major airline on which you have just reserved a flight at the best possible fare. You pick up the phone and call Travel Avenue in Chicago (or any of the growing number of so-called "rebating travel agencies") and tell them what you've got. In exchange for getting the ticket through them, Travel Avenue will write you a check for 5 percent of the domestic fare you've booked or anywhere from 5 percent to 12 percent of any international fare. You get your rebate check along with your ticket.

The folks at Moment's Notice, Adventure International, Mr. Cheap's, and Travel Avenue, are among a small but growing group of entrepreneurial businesspeople who are bringing some time-honored strategies of mass marketing to the travel industry. Later I'll tell you how to get in touch with them and hundreds of other consolidators.

What Is a Consolidator?

In the simplest terms, a consolidator is someone who buys wholesale and sells below retail. In this case, the commodity being purchased is airplane seats. Consolidators buy large blocks of seats from the airlines at steep discounts. They then turn around and sell those seats to you and me (or to travel agents) at a price that is well below the ticket's "face value" but still high enough to earn them a profit.

Why do the airlines sell them this space? For a variety of reasons. For one thing, the airlines reckon they will never sell all their seats at the prices they publish and with the restrictions they place on them. So they sell a portion of their seats to consolidators in the interests of having full, or at least fuller, flights. Selling to consolidators is also a good way for the airlines to raise much-needed cash — now, rather than later. In a sense, the airline is borrowing against its inventory of unsold seats. In exchange for getting paid for next month's flights today, the airline is willing to sell at a discount to the consolidator.

According to travel expert Arthur Frommer, the consolidator movement began in the King's Road section of London where some seedy operations, known as "bucket shops," sprang up in the sixties to serve a growing appetite for affordable travel. From these humble, and somewhat declassé beginnings, consolidators — who disdain the bucket shop label and prefer titles like "bulk fare operators" or "discounters" — have become downright respectable. In fact, some of their best customers are the travel departments of major corporations, which have made a fine art of saving an extra percentage point or two on air fares for their companies' executives.

In today's elastic and highly competitive travel market, the term "consolidator" is used rather loosely. One reason for this is that consolidator tickets can be purchased, for resale, by any travel agent. So perhaps it will be helpful if we refine our definitions somewhat, to cover the entire spectrum of those who deal in below-retail airline tickets. Definitions can get a bit slippery and there are many permutations and combinations, so hang on.

Wholesale consolidators. These are companies that specialize in cutting bulk deals with airlines and then marketing those seats, not to the general public, but to travel agencies, which mark up the ticket and sell it to the ultimate consumer. These companies are probably consolidators in the truest sense.

Retail consolidators. These are companies that make bulk deals with airlines and then sell directly to the public. They might sell tickets to travel agencies as well. Sometimes they will sell tickets to travel agents at a lower fare (called a "net fare") than the one they charge to the public. Sometimes they will sell to the public and to travel agents at the same fare, but then grant the travel agent a commission. Sometimes they will sell to both travel agents and the general public at exactly the same prices; the travel agent, of course, can mark up the ticket he or she purchased. As I use the term, a retail consolidator does little or no business apart from selling the tickets he (they are invariably male in my experience) purchases under contract from the airlines. In other words, retail consolidators are not travel agencies in the generally understood meaning of the term, even though they may have (in fact, usually do have) travel agency accreditation.

Discount travel agencies. Most dealers in consolidator tickets fall into this category. A "discount travel agency" differs from a "full-service travel agency" only to the extent that it positions itself in the marketplace as a source of cheap (or cheaper) travel. These travel agencies can get their consolidator tickets in one of two ways: They can negotiate a contract with an airline or airlines, in which case they would be retail consolidators. Or they can purchase consolidator tickets on an as needed basis from a wholesale or retail consolidator, in which case they are simply functioning as a middleman. Discount travel agencies by their very nature sell a lot of consolidator tickets.

None of this is to suggest, however, that you cannot get a consolidator ticket through a full-service travel agency. Any travel agency can get you a consolidator ticket, although a good many may choose not to do so.

In addition to dealing in consolidator tickets, discount travel agencies offer other savings through such strategies as rebating and selling the wares of low-cost suppliers.

Rebating travel agencies. These days, there is no reason to pay "full-price" (i.e. the price the airline quotes you on the phone) for any airline ticket. A small number of travel agencies are willing to rebate (give back) part of the paltry commission they receive from the airline for booking your ticket. Some agencies advertise this policy, others will rebate if asked, still others will rebate if pressed. Of course, there are a large number of travel agencies that will never rebate, even for their best customers.

In most cases, a rebating agency will not be able to give you the impressive savings of a consolidator ticket. Travel agent commissions are eight percent on domestic flights and not much more on international flights. Airlines have embraced cost-cutting as their mantra and are slashing commission rates and putting $25 to $50 per ticket caps on the commissions they will pay agents. So don't expect to save more than five percent of the ticket price at most from a rebating agency.

Usually, but not always, a rebating travel agent will require that you make the booking with the airline yourself, remembering to ask the airline reservationist for the "record locator number" — a unique alphanumeric code that identifies that specific booking. Then you call the travel agent and relay the particulars of the reservation along with the record locator number. The agency can now go into its computerized reservation system, claim the booking as its own (making it eligible for a commission), and print out the ticket. The agency is willing to rebate five percent to you since you've done most of the work.

Technically speaking, some consolidator fares are the result of rebates from the travel agent to the consumer. Some consolidators sell to travel agents at a fixed price but offer a substantial commission. This commission can be as high as 50 percent for some tickets (usually First or Business Class) on some routes of some foreign flag airlines. If the agent is willing to rebate 40 percent, you've got yourself a good deal. To you, the consumer, of course, this transaction would look like buying any other consolidator ticket — i.e. the travel agent would quote a fare that took into account whatever share of the commission he or she was willing to give back to you, the customer.

As a rough rule of thumb, you will find that travel agencies that deal in consolidator tickets are a good bet to offer modest rebates on non-consolidator tickets.

Charter operators. This is another, separate category of discount travel provider that is often confused with a consolidator. Sometimes agencies that deal in consolidator tickets also deal with charter flights. Often times a charter operator is involved solely in chartering planes, usually to a single destination or a limited number of destinations.

A major, and very important difference between consolidator tickets and charter tickets is that consolidator tickets are for seats on regularly scheduled airlines. Charter tickets, in contrast, are for seats on a single flight of a single aircraft. If the charter operator can't sell enough seats on the flight, he may fold, leaving you holding a worthless ticket. If there is a mechanical problem on the chartered plane, you will sit and wait until it's fixed. That's not to say that a charter cannot be a good budget travel strategy. Just know what you're getting into before turning over your hard earned money.

The companies listed in this book deal primarily in consolidator tickets. They may also deal in charters and may suggest a charter flight to you for a particular destination. Ask to make sure if you have any doubt about what's being offered.

Tour operators. Tour operators put together a number of different pieces — airline tickets, transfers from the airport, hotel accommodations, sightseeing tours — and sell them at a package price. Because they deal in large volumes of airline seats, they often get terrific prices on air which they are willing to pass along to travel agents. A goodly number of tour operators show up in the listings in this book. Obviously travel agents can turn to them for land arrangements as well as air. Tour operators seldom sell directly to the general public.

Sorting it all out. Many times it's hard to know exactly which type of operation you're dealing with. In most cases, it's not important; the result is the same — a cheap ticket. However, sometimes who you are dealing with can make a difference.

- If you are dealing with a retail consolidator, you may get a better deal than you would from a discount agency that is purchasing your ticket from another source. (Then, again, you may not. It's hard to know for sure.)

- On the other hand, a discount travel agency may have more to offer in terms of service and hand-holding. Many consolidators have more in common with old world bazaars, where customer service is an alien concept, than they do with full-service travel agencies that are ready (in theory, at least) to cater to your every whim.

- If you are a travel agent, buying for a client, you will naturally want to cut out as many middlemen as possible. (If you are not a travel agent, I will show you a little later how easy it is to become one and buy consolidator tickets at the special net fares reserved for the trade.)

- If you are a member of the general public, you will find that the wholesale consolidators and tour operators listed here won't deal with you. Either go through your travel agent or become a travel agent yourself (see below, page 22).

What's in It for Me?

In a word — savings! But don't get too excited just yet. Getting the best deal means understanding a little bit about how consolidator fares — and air fares in general — fluctuate.

Air fares vary for a number of reasons. The most familiar cause for changes in fares is time of the year. It's cheaper to fly to

Europe in the winter than it is in the summer. This is true for **all** air ticket markets — the airlines themselves, consolidators, and the air courier companies and other sources I list in my books *Fly Cheap!* and *Air Courier Bargains.* In other words, fares move in tandem regardless of who's offering them.

In the case of consolidator tickets, you probably won't find any great savings on international fares during the off-season. During the high season, however, you can expect savings of 2 percent to 30 percent off the airlines' cheapest advertised fares. This applies to tickets purchased well in advance. If you have to buy a ticket on short notice, your savings will be considerable regardless of the time of year.

Another reason ticket prices vary is clout. The large American airlines that service Europe, for example, have market share. They advertise heavily; they have brand recognition, frequent flyer inducements, and so forth. They also have a good selection of flights. For all of these advantages, they command a higher price. What many people don't know is that there are other, smaller, foreign carriers flying to interesting European destinations. They don't have market share, frequent flyer programs, or many flights each week. One result is that they offer some surprising bargains, especially through consolidators, several of whom specialize in these lesser-known carriers.

Convenience is another factor in air fares. It makes sense that a nonstop flight to, say, London will be more expensive than a flight that stops in Glasgow, Scotland, first. Or that a flight to Paris will cost more than a flight to Luxembourg with a stopover in Iceland. Consolidators can be an excellent source of bargains on airlines that have odd routes or "inconvenient" connections.

Still another factor is demand. High summer fares is one example of how demand affects price. But there are other factors that can come into play. During the war in the Gulf in the early nineties, travelers deserted Europe in droves, creating bargains galore for those who were unafraid of Sadaam Hussein's terrorists — who, it turned out, never attacked a single plane! Not a single American tourist was injured in Europe during the Gulf war. Remember that the next time your fellow vacationers get cold feet because of some international "incident."

Another factor affecting fares is the increasing regularity of "fare wars" in which airlines try to grab market share (or some much needed cash) by announcing very attractive fares for a limited period of time. One little known result of fare wars is that they can suddenly render consolidator fares uncompetitive. The reason is that the price negotiated by the consolidator, once negotiated, remains fixed for the duration of the contract. If a competing airline's fares (or even the fares on the airline with which the consolidator is dealing) drop, that's the consolidator's misfortune. Fares wars don't invariably undercut consolidator fares, but it does happen.

To sum it up, consolidators make the most sense:

- *In the high-season,* when ticket prices are normally inflated because of increased demand. If you are planning a family vacation abroad, consolidators will provide your best bet. Get some idea of what's available through the airlines, tour packages, etc. Then, shop aggressively for the best consolidator fare.

- *When you have to fly on short notice.* Unless you can get a last-minute courier bargain, consolidators are your best bet for savings. They can offer substantially lower prices than the airlines will charge you for a ticket purchased after the super-saver deadline. Be aware, however, of the differences between courier companies and consolidators. As the flight date approaches, the courier company gets more and more nervous that they'll have no one to fill that seat; consequently the fare goes down to lure someone into taking it. For a consolidator, on the other hand, a ticket becomes, if anything, more valuable as the flight date approaches. That's because the consolidator knows his best customers are those people who must purchase tickets at short notice. So don't expect the phenomenal deals you can get from the courier companies. Expect instead to pay a fare somewhere close to the super-saver fare you might have gotten had you been able to book the flight earlier. Some consolidators specialize in selling seats only on flights that are leaving in fewer than 30 days.

14

- *When you're looking for an offbeat, bargain vacation.* There are some excellent deals to be had if you're willing to go off the beaten track — say to Turkey or Romania. The listings later in this book will point you to consolidators who specialize in or highlight specific destinations.
- *When you're looking at a high-priced trip.* If you are planning to go around the world or want to take six family members along on a shorter trip, even a small savings percentage-wise can be worth a few hundred dollars to you.

Tradeoffs

As with so much in this life, consolidator discounts aren't always a perfect solution for everybody in every circumstance. Here are some things that may (or may not) be negatives, depending on your needs and preferences.

- Don't expect any great deals on First Class or Business Class tickets. A few consolidators "specialize" in these seats but the discounts are not the greatest. Feel lucky if you get as much as 10 percent off. Every once in a while you may be able to save as much as 20 percent. By and large, though, the consolidator market is strictly coach.
- Many consolidators deal with foreign airlines. As a travel agent, I have discovered that some people just don't feel comfortable unless they are flying a major U.S. or European airline. If you are one of these people, your choice of consolidator tickets will be somewhat more limited. You will also most likely pay a bit more. Many of the foreign carriers used by consolidators are every bit as professional, safety conscious, and reliable as their American counterparts. Others, notably those from some of the former Iron Curtain countries, have had their problems. Use your discretion and fly on airlines on which you will feel safe and comfortable. You will always know what airline you'll

be on before you buy the ticket.

- You're locked in to the airline on the ticket. Very few consolidator tickets allow you to change airlines.
- Refunds aren't always available and, if they are, they are available only through the consolidator.
- You may have to pay by check, or even cash, denying you the extra security that comes with using a credit card. A growing number of consolidators take plastic, but using it may add a bit to your fare.
- True consolidators are small, independent operators, usually operating on wafer thin margins. Concepts like "total customer service" don't compute in these circumstances. So don't expect high levels of service. Also, some consolidators are recent immigrants who are better at shaving an extra dollar off a fare than they are at speaking English. What you interpret as rudeness may simply be a language barrier. All that being said, most consolidators (there are exceptions, of course) are honest. Once you get used to the peculiarities of this corner of the travel marketplace, you should have no problems.

Many airlines, especially the big ones, treat consolidator tickets (and the passengers holding them) differently from "regular" tickets (and ticketholders). Most of these limitations are minor and will be unimportant to the vast majority of budget travelers who, after all, are more than willing to accept a few tradeoffs for a lower fare.

Here is a checklist of common restrictions or tradeoffs that may — repeat, may — apply to some consolidator tickets. When planning your trip, determine if any of these things are important to you. If so, let the consolidator know. He may be able to accommodate you. Just be aware that you may be missing out on a lower fare to get the added "convenience."

- Do I need to get frequent flyer miles for this trip?
- Do I want to have advance seating assignment?
- Do I need a direct flight (as opposed to making a connection)?
- Will I require a special meal during the flight?

- If there's a delay, will I need free meals or a room?
- Will I need a refundable ticket in case my plans change?

Frequent flyer mileage is an issue for some travelers. Of course, if you're flying on an obscure Eastern European or Middle Eastern airline, you probably wouldn't have much use for their frequent flyer miles anyway. Nonetheless, many consolidator tickets are sold on U.S. flag carriers or their so-called "travel partners" that do offer frequent flyer miles. Why then can you get them with some consolidator tickets and not with others? The answer lies in the nature of the ticket you are buying. If you are purchasing a ticket that has been obtained at a "net fare," it may have attached to it a fare code that precludes frequent flyer miles. Remember that frequent flyer miles are, themselves, a form of discount or rebate. When the cost of a ticket drops below a certain point, the airline figures it doesn't pay to offer frequent flyer miles in addition to the low fare, and the fare code attached to that ticket reflects that reasoning.

As noted earlier, however, some consolidator fares are actually the result of a rebate of part of the agent's commission. Some agencies, because of the large volume of business they bring to certain airlines, qualify for "overrides" or extra-large commissions. These commissions can go as high as 30 or 40 percent. In this case, the ticket is actually fairly high-priced. The savings you realize comes about because the agent doesn't take the entire commission to which he's entitled.

One way to tell which kind of ticket you have is to look at the fare box on the ticket itself. If it says "bulk" or "coach" or otherwise has no specific dollar amount, you probably have a consolidator ticket sold at a net fare. If there is a dollar figure on the ticket, higher than the price you paid, you have most likely received a rebate of the agent's override.

Some travelers are just as concerned about the comfort of the trip as they are with the price of the ticket. If you are among these folks, you will have to balance your savings against the length of the trip. Many consolidator tickets are cheaper in part because they involve flights that stop several times or require a change of planes and/or a roundabout routing. Sometimes you will have to choose between consolidator alternatives. For example, you might be able to fly from New York to Harare via London at a consolidator fare of $1200 or $1300 on a world-class airline. Or you could opt to fly on an Eastern European flag carrier, with a stopover in Sofia, for just $900. One fare is cheaper, but the flight is a good bit longer and involves a change of planes.

Another tradeoff in the consolidator arena is the fact that it remains largely a marketplace for international tickets. A growing number of consolidators are offering seats on domestic U.S. flights but they are still a minority. Moreover, the domestic flights that are available tend to be popular, long-haul routes — New York to Hawaii, Seattle to Miami, and so forth. Still, bargains are sometimes available on shorter hauls; it never hurts to ask.

Dealing with Consolidators

The easiest way to deal with a consolidator is to use your nearest full-service travel agent instead! This assumes, of course, that you have established a good, on-going relationship with a knowledgeable travel agent who is committed to getting you the lowest possible fares in exchange for having your business year in, year out — including some business on which he or she can make a comfortable margin.

As noted earlier, many consolidators, including the country's largest, are strictly wholesale and will not deal directly with the public. So going through a travel agent automatically gives you access to a bigger market. And any travel agent can deal with any consolidator. If your travel agent refuses to get you a consolidator ticket, you obviously have not yet found the right travel agent.

Another reason to deal with a local travel agent is the sheer convenience. You make one call and you can often pick up the ticket (and pay for it) close to flight time. Also, a good travel agent will get to know your preferences and your needs. You will only have to outline the dos and don'ts one time. In addition, your local travel agent may be more knowledgeable about buying consolidator tickets and less likely to get you into a bad deal. This is not a universal rule, of course. Not all travel agents are equally knowledgeable.

Of course, you should expect to pay a little more through a full-service travel agent. That's only fair. Nonetheless, a consolidator ticket purchased through a travel agent should cost a good bit less than a non-consolidator ticket — otherwise what's the point?

Chances are that you are a bit more adventurous than that. After all, why did you invest in this book? The listings provided later will give you all the information you need to get closer to the consolidator market on your own. You can often get a better deal that way and, if you are an avid shopper, there's the thrill of the chase.

In fact, many consolidators are very much like your local travel agent anyway. That is, you can pick up the phone, tell them what you want, book a flight, pay for it with a credit card, and have it mailed to you. Location is not a problem (if time is not a factor) and many consolidators have toll-free 800 numbers. However, you may want to look for a consolidator close to you for the added convenience of local pickup.

Just make sure you have organized all the information about dates and destinations and anything else you want the consolidator to know before you start making calls. If you are looking for the absolute cheapest fare, even if it means making connections, be sure to let the consolidator know. And don't forget about hotels at your destination. Many consolidators can get you discounts on your hotel stay. Some will sell you discounted hotel rooms even if you don't get your ticket from them! Ask.

How to detect a bait and switch scam. Some unscrupulous discounters or consolidators will advertise super-cheap fares in the newspaper. When you call to reserve your flight, however, you find that the low-low fare isn't available for that date or has been sold out. Of course, the discounter will be happy to sell you a ticket at a higher price. Now in all fairness, they might be telling you the truth. Planes get booked solid and there are only a limited number of seats per flight at a given fare.

If you try a few other dates and get the same story, however, you should be suspicious. If the consolidator cannot confirm a seat at the advertised fare on any date, then the evidence that they are engaging in bait and switch is overwhelming. Hang up and complain to the Better Business Bureau and your state's Attorney General.

Getting the best deal. Nothing beats concerted comparison shopping. But doing a little advance research can be invaluable. After all, you have no way of knowing how good the "discount" price is unless you know the "regular" price. Begin by calling a few airlines directly to inquire about fares. Then try some local full-service travel agencies, asking for the "best" fare they can give you. Skipping this step might cost you money.

Don't assume that the ticket you get from a consolidator will automatically be a better deal than you could get from the airline. Airlines often slash ticket prices (during a fare war, for example) below the prices a consolidator can offer (see page 14). Sometimes an airline will offer a special promotional fare for a brief time on a certain route. Always check the retail price before looking for bargains.

Once you have an idea of the "fair market value" of the ticket you're looking for, use the listings in this book and start making calls. Get several quotes before deciding on the best deal. Don't allow yourself to be pressured into making a commitment before you're ready. After a few calls, you'll get the hang of it.

If you are a travel agent, you will naturally be looking for wholesalers. In theory, that's where you'll get the best deal. However, some consolidators sell to travel agents and the public at the same fares.

If you are a travel agent, you owe it to yourself to take out a subscription to the oddly named *Jax Fax*. This monthly "travel marketing magazine" is the size of a small town's phone book and lists consolidator fares being offered to the trade. They are conveniently broken down by destination.

In fact, even if you're not a travel agent, you might want to consider subscribing to *Jax Fax* because it is so cheap. As I write this, *Jax Fax* is offering a two-year subscription for just $24. That's a small price to pay for a magazine that could save you hundreds if not thousands of dollars. (*Jax Fax,* 397 Post Road, P.O. Box 4013, Darien, CT 06820-1413, 800-952-9329.)

Jax Fax will let you know the "going rate," the net fares consolidators are offering to travel agents for destinations in which you are interested. As a consumer, you may not be able to get those fares, but they will serve as an indicator of how close you are getting to wholesale. Of course, after you finish reading this book, you may decide it's worth your while to become a travel agent and qualify for the net fares yourself.

Round-the-world. Special mention should be made of "around-the-world" and "circle Pacific" fares. If you are looking at a long trip — say New York to Australia — you might find that, through a consolidator, you can continue on from Australia, visiting India and Europe, for about the same price (or even less) than the regular round-trip fare. Circle Pacific routes work the same way, letting you fly from Los Angeles or San Francisco to places like Hong Kong, Australia, Fiji, and back. *Jax Fax* regularly lists consolidators offering these tempting options.

Risks and Remedies

I am often asked, "Are consolidators reliable?" Well, sure, some consolidators go out of business. But then so do some airlines! The fact is, nothing's for certain. And I'm certainly not going to guarantee that nothing awful will happen to you if you call one of the companies listed in this book. On the other hand, they've all been around for a while and they have all sold thousands and thousands of tickets to people who had perfectly uneventful trips. So the odds are in your favor. Nonetheless, there are some precautions you can take if you're the nervous type:

Use a credit card to pay for your ticket. Not all consolidators take credit cards. Of those that do, most will add a surcharge of 2 percent to 5 percent to cover the fee the credit card company charges them. The advantage of using a credit card is that you can stop payment if the ticket you receive is not the ticket you agreed on with the consolidator. The small extra cost may be worth the added security.

Find a consolidator close to home. That way you can visit in person and reassure yourself that these are people you feel comfortable doing business with. Also, if something does go wrong, you'll have a desk to pound on.

Take out travel insurance. Since consolidator tickets are invariably non-refundable, if you get sick or have to cancel or change your plans for any reason, you can be out a bundle. Trip cancellation insurance can soften (if not eliminate) the blow. Just make sure you read the fine print and understand the restrictions.

Ask to get your tickets as soon as possible. Again, the idea is that if something is wrong, you'll have time to get it fixed. If it's too close to flight time, you may face the choice of using the ticket as is or canceling the trip. Another way of saying the same thing is resist making full payment until you receive the tickets. If you are dealing with a local consolidator, don't turn over payment until you've had a chance to examine the tickets and make sure everything is as agreed.

Beware of altered tickets. Examine handwritten tickets for any signs of erasures or changes. If it's a computer generated ticket, look for stickers used to change the information in various fields. Erasures may render the ticket invalid and stickers are not allowed on tickets issued by American travel agencies. Talk to the consolidator; check with the airline; make sure you have a valid ticket.

Beware of coupon deals. Sometimes the eye-popping fare being offered is tied to using a frequent flyer coupon that has been sold by its rightful owner. This is especially true of deep-discount offers in First Class and Business Class. The airlines say these coupons are non-transferable; others maintain that the free market is the free market. If you get caught, however, the airline can (and most often does) refuse to board you unless you pay the full unrestricted fare. So unless you are prepared to take on the airlines in court and pay full fare in the meantime, steer clear of these shady deals.

Becoming a Travel Agent

The best way to get the best fares in the consolidator market is to become a travel agent. Before you start saying you don't have the time to go to travel school or the tens of thousands of dollars to post a bond, let me assure you that there is a way to become a travel agent, legally and ethically, without investing big bucks.

I did it and I did it for well under $100 dollars — including business cards!

The secret is to become an outside sales representative for a travel agency that *does* have all the proper accreditation and *has* posted the huge bond. It's even possible to hook up with an agency that has its own in-house consolidator, as I did.

Becoming an outside sales rep allows you to collect commissions on certain types of travel transactions. For example, as a private individual, you can make an airline reservation for your Aunt Martha but you cannot sell her the ticket or collect a commission on it. You can book Aunt Martha into the Hilton at her destination and call Avis to arrange to have a rental car waiting for her. But neither Hilton or Avis will send you a commission check. As an outside rep for a bona-fide travel agency, however, you can do all of the above *and* get a commission. In the case of Aunt Martha's airline ticket, the agency prints the ticket, collects the commission and splits it with you. In the case of the hotel and car reservations, Hilton and Avis forward the commission to the agency, and the agency splits it with you.

How the commission is split between the agency and the outside rep is a matter of negotiation and contract. Typical splits range from 50 percent to 80 percent. (That is, the outside rep receives 50 to 80 percent of the commission.)

There are some types of travel sales that *don't* have to be funneled through an agency, however, and consolidator tickets are one of them. As an outside agent, I have dealt directly with a number of consolidators, always paying net fares and marking up the tickets as I saw fit. I have also purchased tickets for my own use. There's no reason you can't do the same.

There are some practical considerations to bear in mind if you are going to implement this strategy. First of all, consolidators who sell to travel agents at net fare rates have an obvious vested interest in assuring themselves that the travel agents to whom they sell are, in fact, travel agents. If they sell to travel agents and the general public at different prices, they want to keep the two categories separate. (Of course, if they sell to the general public and travel agents *at the same price*, they don't care whether you are a travel agent or not.) If they sell only to travel agents, they have an obvious interest in controlling to whom they sell. If it were to become known that they were selling directly to the public (even if unintentionally), their regular customers would be understandably annoyed.

The question then becomes, how does a consolidator determine that you are a travel agent? There are several ways your identity as an agent can be established:

- **You tell them you're a travel agent.** I strongly suspect that, as long as the check or credit card number is good or you pay in cash, many consolidators don't really care if you're an agent or not. As the saying goes, "If it looks like a duck and quacks like a duck . . ." Some consolidators will be more stringent than others in checking out your status. Of course, if the name on the ticket and the name of the agent booking it are the same, that's a pretty obvious tip-off that you might not be an agent.
- **You pay by agency check.** Your business check has your business name printed right on the check. If your business name is Sam's Travel, no problem. If your business name is Sam's Dry Cleaners, potential problem. If your business name is Sam's Enterprises, you may be given the benefit of the doubt.
- **You actually are a travel agent.** This is far and away the best alternative. You have a business checking account in the name of your travel business. You are affiliated with a travel agency as an outside rep. You have business cards. You buy the occasional consolidator ticket for clients. You have no legal, moral, or ethical worries. And since it's so easy, so cheap, and so much fun to become a travel agent, why not go ahead and do it?

Can you finesse a consolidator into thinking you're a travel agent, even when you're not? Probably. Many of these transactions are done over the phone, using credit cards, and it's not unheard of for agency owners to get consolidator tickets for their own use or use their own credit cards to make purchases. I wouldn't advise pretending to be something you're not, however. Go ahead and do it right.

Making money with consolidator tickets. As a *real* travel agent, you can earn money selling travel that you can put to use paying for your own next trip. An excellent way to do that is to buy consolidator tickets for friends, family, or neighbors at the net fare and add on a markup. Consolidator tickets seldom if ever have the actual price paid marked on them. In the fare box it will say things like "bulk" or "coach" or list the much higher full coach fare. So your customer has no way of knowing what you actually paid for the ticket. And it's only fair you should be compensated for your time and effort in researching and obtaining this great deal for your customer.

Here's a painless strategy for buying and selling consolidator tickets. Tell your friends to go out and find the best deal they can get and tell them that if you can beat it you will, if not, then they know they're getting the best price. When they come back with the fare, check with your favorite consolidators (or consult *Jax Fax*). If you can beat the fare, split the savings with your friend. In other words, if you can get the ticket for $100 less, sell it for $50 less. It's a win-win proposition for both parties.

Once a consolidator knows you buy for others, he will not question the fact that you buy tickets for yourself as well.

Becoming an outside travel agent is surprisingly easy. I tell exactly how to go about it — and how to build a profitable part-time business for yourself — in my book, *Home-Based Travel Agent: How To Cash In On The Exciting NEW World Of Travel Marketing*. At 400 pages, the book explains the ins and outs and profit opportunities of selling travel in much more detail than I have space for here.

If you'd like to explore this avenue more fully, use the order form at the back of this book. Or visit the Home-Based Travel Agent Resource Center on the Internet at http://www.intrepidtraveler.com/homebased/.

Chapter Two

Consolidators in the U.S. and Canada

The following list is arranged alphabetically, by company name, U.S. state or Canadian province, and city. In subsequent chapters, consolidators are sorted and cross-referenced in a variety of ways to make it as easy as possible for you to find what you need. The following information is provided:

Name: In some cases, the full name has been abbreviated for space considerations.

800 #: The toll-free number, if any. Be aware that some toll-free numbers may not be accessible from all locations.

Local #: The consolidator's local telephone number. Note that area codes are changing rapidly in some regions. If you dial a number and get the message that you have reached a nonworking number, you may want to contact information to see if the area code has changed. Simply dial the area code plus 555-1212.

City and State (or Province): The city and state or Canadian province in which the consolidator is located. Standard postal abbreviations are used for the state and province designations. Usually, a consolidator's location is not an overriding factor. If you want a flight out of Chicago, say, you don't necessarily have to deal with a Chicago consolidator. Many consolidators can provide tickets on flights departing from many different cities. You can make arrangements over the phone and have the tickets mailed or expressed to you. A few consolidators, however, specialize only in tickets leaving from the city in which they are located or from nearby cities. In addition, you may find it more convenient or reassuring to deal with a consolidator whose office you can visit.

Sells To: "T" indicates the consolidator sells only to travel agents. "P" indicates that the consolidator sells to the general public. "B" indicates that the consolidator sells to both travel agents and the public; usually, but not always, this means that the consolidator sells to travel agents at a different, lower, fare.

Also, some of the companies listed are tour operators that sell consolidator tickets only to travel agents, but will sell tour packages to the general public.

Web Site: If the company has a web site, it is listed here. Generally, I have avoided listing web sites of companies that do not have their own domain names, on the theory that these web addresses are the most likely to change. You may want to check an Internet search engine such as Yahoo or Alta Vista to see if a company in which you are interested has such a web address or has put up a web site since this book was published.

Notes: The destinations most frequently served by the consolidator and other pertinent facts are provided under each listing. Scan these notes to locate the most likely consolidators for your trip. When the consolidator serves only a limited number of countries or cities within a given area, such as Asia, I indicate that by putting the countries or cities served in parentheses following the area. For example, "Asia (Japan)" means the consolidator handles tickets to Japan. In contrast, "Asia, Japan" without parentheses would mean the consolidator specializes in Japan but also sells tickets to other destinations in Asia.

Note that "worldwide" means international destinations only. I add the designation "US" when a consolidator sells domestic tickets.

Abbreviations: RWT - 'round the world. CIS - Confederation of Independent States, the now-independent countries that were formerly parts of the USSR. C. & S. America - Central and South America.

In the following list, each entry is arranged as follows:

Company	800 # Website Notes	Local #	City	State	Sells To
1-800-Airfare	800-247-3273 www.800airfare.com Europe, Asia, S. America, US/ Canada	610-834-8150	Plymouth Mtg	PA	B
1-800-FLYCHEAP	800-359-24327 US		San Diego	CA	P
2000 Latin Tours	800-254-7378 C. & S. America	305-670-4488	Miami	FL	B
4th Dimension Tours	800-343-0020 www.4thdimension.com Europe, S. America	305-279-0014	Miami	FL	B
A Affordable Travel	800-658-4366 www.affordabletravel.kearney.net Africa	308-234-2824	Kearney	NE	T
Abratours	800-227-2887 Middle East (Israel, Egypt, Jordan), Europe (Greece)	914-949-3300	White Plains	NY	B
Accent on Africa	888-237-4230 www.accentonafrica.com Africa	860-355-5800	Watertown	CT	B
Adventure Bound Tours	www.adventure-bound.com Worldwide	602-968-7889	Tempe	AZ	B
Adventure Int'l Travel Service	800-542-2487 Europe (Eastern)	216-228-7171	Lakewood	OH	B
AESU Travel	800-638-7640 www.aesu.com Europe, student groups	410-366-5494	Baltimore	MD	B
Affinity Travel	888-733-4726 www.irantravel.com Middle East (Iran, the Gulf)	303-639-1000	Denver	CO	B
African Travel	800-421-8907 www.africantravelinc.com Africa	818-507-7893	Glendale	CA	T
Agents Advantage	800-816-2211 Europe, Latin America, US	908-355-2222	West Orange	NJ	T
Air Brokers International	800-883-3273 www.airbrokers.com RTW, Asia, Circle Pacific, Australia, hotels	415-397-1383	San Francisco	CA	B

Air Discounters International	800-527-2589	972-980-4540	Dallas	TX	P
	www.airdiscounters.com				
	Worldwide. Use ext. 129				
Air Tickets	800-207-7300	212-557-3275	New York	NY	T
	www.airtickets.com				
	Worldwide (exc. S. America)				
Air Travel Discounts	800-888-2621	310-289-9761	Beverly Hills	CA	B
		561-794-9345	Vero Beach	FL	
		212-922-1326	New York	NY	
	www.airdisc.com				
	Europe, Middle East, Asia, Africa				
Air-Supply		212-695-1647	New York	NY	P
	www.air-supply.com				
	Europe, Africa, S.E. Asia, Australia				
Airbound		415-834-9445	San Francisco	CA	P
	Worldwide				
Airfare Busters	800-232-8783	713-961-5109	Houston	TX	B
	www.afbusters.com				
	Worldwide				
Airfares	800-753-0578	212-213-3865	New York	NY	B
	members.aol.com/airfares4				
	Europe (Central & Eastern)				
Airmakers	800-841-4321	206-216-2914	Seattle	WA	T
	www.airmakers.com				
	Worldwide (exc. S. Pacific)				
Airplan	800-866-7526	412-257-3199	Pittsburgh	PA	T
	www.airplan.com				
	Europe, Africa, Asia, S. America, Middle East				
AIT/Anderson Int'l Travel	800-365-1929	517-337-1300	East Lansing	MI	T
	Europe, Africa				
All Continents Travel	800-368-6822	310-337-1641	Los Angeles	CA	P
	www.ptla.com/allcontinents				
	Europe, Africa, Middle East, C. America (Mexico)				
All Destinations	800-228-1510	203-744-3100	Ridgefield	CT	B
	www.alldestinations.com				
	Caribbean, US, C. & S. America				
Aloha Continental Travel	800-287-0275	714-565-3737	Santa Ana	CA	B
	www.alohacontinental.com				
	Europe, US				
Alp Reyal Tours	800-853-3058	504-488-4146	New Orleans	LA	B
	877-988-8802	732-988-8814	Bradley Beach	NJ	
	Europe, Mediterranean				

Alpha Travel	800-793-8424	770-988-9982	Marietta	GA B
	www.alpha4travel.com			
	US, Europe, Africa, Middle East			
Alta Tours	800-338-4191	415-777-1307	San Francisco	CA B
	www.altatours.com			
	Europe (Spain, Portugal), S. America (Argentina, Chile)			
Amba Travel		212-868-2500	New York	NY P
	Europe, Asia (India)			
Am-Jet Travels	800-414-4147	212-697-5332	New York	NY B
	www.nbic.org/amjet			
	Middle East, India, Asia, US, last minute, one-way			
American Int'l Consolidators	800-888-5774	914-682-5679	Hartsdale	NY T
	www.aictravel.com			
	Europe, US			
American Media Tours (AMT)	800-969-6344	212-465-1630	New York	NY B
	www.americanmediatours.com			
	Europe (France, Russia), Caribbean, US			
American Travel		216-781-7181	Cleveland	OH B
	Europe			
American Travel Abroad	800-228-0877	212-586-5230	New York	NY T
	www.amta.com			
	Europe (Eastern)			
Americas Tours	800-553-2513	206-623-8850	Seattle	WA P
	C. & S. America, hotels, tours			
Americas Travel Services	800-704-6484	202-955-3815	Washington	DC B
	C. & S. America			
ANA Hallo Tours	800-421-4136	212-399-6286	New York	NY B
	Asia (Japan)			
APC	800-933-4421	323-655-6121	Los Angeles	CA T
	888-971-0006	212-972-1558	New York	NY
	Worldwide, US, TWA			
APF Inc.	800-888-9168	626-282-9988	Alhambra	CA B
	Asia			
Apple Vacations	800-800-0202	408-452-0202	San Jose	CA T
	800-365-2776	847-640-1150	Elk Grove Vlg	IL
	800-727-3400	610-359-6700	Philadelphia	PA
	www.applevacations.com			
	Hawaii, Caribbean, C. America (Mexico)			
Ariel Tours, Inc.	800-262-1818	718-633-7900	Brooklyn	NY T
	www.arieltours.com			
	Middle East (Israel)			

31

Arkia Travel		212-557-1587	New York	NY	B
	Worldwide, US				
Around the World Travel	800-766-3601	206-223-3600	Seattle	WA	B
	www.netfares.net				
	RTW, Europe, Asia , India, Africa, S. America				
Arrow Travel		212-889-2550	New York	NY	P
	Worldwide				
Asia Specialists	800-969-7427	703-941-2323	Annandale	VA	B
	Asia				
Asia Travel Service		808-944-8811	Honolulu	HI	B
	Asia, US				
Asian Travel	800-334-2742	602-954-0101	Phoenix	AZ	T
	Asia, (sells to public in AZ)				
ATC Travel	800-826-6388	212-967-1200	New York	NY	B
	C. & S. America, Europe				
Aus Travel	800-633-3404	415-781-4329	San Francisco	CA	P
		954-525-6440	Ft. Lauderdale	FL	
		212-972-6880	New York	NY	
	Australia, N. Zealand, S. Pacific				
Ausbound	800-345-5877		Seattle	WA	T
	Australia, N. Zealand, S. Pacific, US				
Avanti Destinations	800-422-4256	503-295-1998	Portland	OR	T
	Europe, C. & S. America, Asia				
Avia Travel	800-950-2842	415-536-4155	San Francisco	CA	P
	www.avia.com				
	Asia, RTW				
Aviation Travels & Tours		201-418-8167	Jersey City	NJ	P
	Worldwide				
Azure Travel Bureau	800-882-1427	212-252-1056	New York	NY	B
	www.azuretravel.com				
	India, Nepal, Asia (Tibet)				
B & D Tours	800-548-6877	212-953-3300	New York	NY	B
	Middle East (Israel)				
Balkan USA	800-822-1106	212-338-6838	New York	NY	B
	www.balkanusa.com				
	Europe (Bulgaria & Romania)				
Benyo World Travel	800-872-8925	914-968-0175	Yonkers	NY	B
	www.benyo.com				
	Europe (Eastern)				
Best Travel	800-709-4545	703-924-9590	Alexandria	VA	T
	S.E. Asia				

Bethany Travel Agency		202-223-3336	Washington	DC B
	Worldwide (exc. C. America)			
Blaney's Travel Plus	800-376-6177	250-382-7254	Victoria	BC P
	blaneystravel.com			
	Europe, US/Canada, C. America (Mexico)			
Blueskies Travel	800-538-7597	256-551-1775	Huntsville	AL B
	www.blueskiestravel.com			
	Europe, Africa, S. Asia, Australia			
Borgsmiller Travels	800-228-0585	618-529-5511	Carbondale	IL B
	www.mta-tvl.com			
	Asia (Malaysia)			
Brazil Tours	800-927-8352	818-990-4995	Sherman Oaks	CA B
	www.braziltours.com			
	S. America			
Brazilian Travel Service	800-342-5746	212-764-6161	New York	NY B
	S. America, US, Worldwide			
Brazilian Wave Tours & Travel	800-682-3315	954-561-3788	Ft. Lauderdale	FL B
	S. America, Brazil			
Brendan Air	800-491-9633	818-785-9696	Van Nuys	CA T
	www.brendantours.com			
	Worldwide			
Butte Travel Service	800-661-8906	780-477-3561	Edmonton	AB P
	www.buttetravel.ab.ca			
	Europe, Caribbean, Hawaii, (serves Western Canada)			
C & H International	800-833-8888	323-933-2288	Los Angeles	CA T
	800-289-1628	415-956-2288	San Francisco	CA
		202-223-2288	Washington	DC
		312-346-2828	Chicago	IL
		617-357-1608	Boston	MA
		212-219-9300	New York	NY
	888-440-2288	713-272-0006	Houston	TX
	888-808-2288		Seattle	WA
	www.cnhintl.com			
	Worldwide			
Calcos Tours		212-889-9200	New York	NY B
	S. America (Argentina, Brazil, Chile, Uraguay)			
Campus Travel	800-328-3359	612-338-5616	Minneapolis	MN B
	Europe fr. Minneapolis			
Cannetic Travel	888-279-9902	604-279-0066	Richmond	BC B
	Asia (China)			

Carbone Travel	800-735-8899	212-213-4310	New York	NY	B
	www.carbone-travel.com				
	S. America				
Carefree Getaway Travel	800-969-8687	817-430-5828	Trophy Club	TX	B
	www.carefree.com				
	Europe, Asia, US				
Caribbean Tours Specialists	800-930-9021	516-827-9884	Jericho	NY	T
	Caribbean				
Cathay Travel		626-571-6727	Monterey Park	CA	B
	Asia (Hong Kong, Indonesia), Canada, Worldwide				
Central Europe Holidays	800-800-8891	212-725-0948	New York	NY	B
	members.aol.com/ceheurope				
	Europe (Eastern)				
Central Holidays Tours	800-935-5000	310-216-5777	Los Angeles	CA	T
	800-935-5000	201-228-5200	Englew'd Cliffs	NJ	B
	www.centralh.com				
	Mediterranean, ski packages to Europe & US/Canada				
Central Travel Network		714-520-4535	Anaheim	CA	B
		619-239-9090	San Diego	CA	
		415-285-0288	San Francisco	CA	
		818-785-8844	Van Nuys	CA	
		312-368-8288	Chicago	IL	
		708-656-1190	Cicero	IL	
		702-388-1663	Las Vegas	NV	
		214-943-5400	Dallas	TX	
	Hawaii, C. & S. America				
Centrav, Inc.	800-874-2033	612-948-8400	Minneapolis	MN	T
	Worldwide (exc. Caribbean)				
CES Travel	800-222-3020	312-922-2994	Chicago	IL	T
	Africa				
Chad & Calden		514-729-0111	Montreal	PQ	P
	www.chad-calden.com				
	Worldwide				
Charterways	800-869-2344	408-257-2652	San Jose	CA	T
	Worldwide				
Cheap Seats	800-451-7200	818-717-8591	Los Angeles	CA	P
	Europe, C. & S. America				
Cheap Seats	888-221-2727	303-338-5558	Aurora	CO	B
	www.cheapseatsinc.com				
	US				

Cheap Tickets	800-377-1000		Lakeport	CA	P
		310-645-5054	Los Angeles	CA	
		808-947-3717	Honolulu	HI	
		212-570-1179	New York	NY	
	www.cheaptickets.com				
	Worldwide				
China Professional Tours	800-252-4462	770-849-0300	Norcross	GA	B
	www.chinaprofessional.com				
	S.E. Asia				
China Travel Service	800-899-8618	415-352-8618	San Francisco	CA	P
	Asia, hotels, charters				
Chisholm Travel	800-631-2824	312-321-1800	Chicago	IL	P
	www.chisholmair.net				
	Asia, S. Pacific				
City Tours OBT	800-238-2489	201-939-6572	Rutherford S. America	NJ	T
	www.citytours.com/obt				
Cloud Tours Travel	800-223-7880	212-753-6104	New York	NY	B
	www.cloudtours.com				
	Europe (Greece)				
Club America Travel	800-221-4969	212-972-2865	New York	NY	B
	www.clubamericatravel.com				
	Middle East (Turkish Airlines)				
CMM Travel	800-458-6663	212-557-1530	New York	NY	T
	Asia				
Compare Travel	800-532-9939	312-853-1144	Chicago	IL	T
	www.cl.ais.net/compare				
	Worldwide (exc. C. & S. America)				
Continental Travel Shop		310-453-8655	Santa Monica	CA	B
	Europe				
Cosmopolitan Travel Center	800-548-7206	954-523-0973	Ft. Lauderdale	FL	T
	Europe, S. America, land packages in Turkey				
Council Travel	800-226-8624	(nat'l res. ctr.)	Boston	MA	P
		602-966-3544	Tempe	AZ	
		520-881-8345	Tucson	AZ	
		510-848-8604	Berkeley*	CA	
		530-752-2285	Davis	CA	
		209-278-6623	Fresno	CA	
		714-278-2157	Fullerton	CA	
		805-562-8080	Isla Vista	CA	
		619-452-0630	La Jolla	CA	

Council Travel
(cont'd)

562-621-6603	Long Beach*	CA
310-208-3551	Los Angeles*	CA
818-882-4692	Northridge	CA
650-325-3888	Palo Alto*	CA
626-793-5595	Pasadena	CA
916-278-4224	Sacramento	CA
619-270-6401	San Diego*	CA
415-421-3473	San Francisco*	CA
805-562-8080	Santa Barb.*	CA
303-447-8101	Boulder	CO
303-571-0630	Denver	CO
203-562-5335	New Haven*	CT
202-337-6464	Washington*	DC
305-670-9261	Miami*	FL
404-377-9997	Atlanta*	GA
515-296-2326	Ames	IA
312-951-0585	Chicago	IL
847-475-5070	Evanston	IL
812-330-1600	Bloomington*	IN
785-749-3900	Lawrence	KS
504-866-1767	New Orleans	LA
413-256-1261	Amherst*	MA
617-266-1926	Boston*	MA
617-497-1497	Cambridge*	MA
410-516-0560	Baltimore*	MD
301-779-1172	College Park*	MD
734-998-0200	Ann Arbor*	MI
517-432-7722	East Lansing	MI
612-379-2323	Minneapolis	MN
919-942-2334	Chapel Hill*	NC
732-249-6667	New Brunsw'k	NC
607-277-0373	Ithaca	NY
212-666-4177	New York	NY
212-254-2525	New York	NY
212-822-2700	New York*	NY
614-294-8697	Columbus	OH
541-344-2263	Eugene	OR
503-228-1900	Portland*	OR
215-382-0343	Philadelphia*	PA
412-683-1881	Pittsburgh	PA
814-861-3232	State College*	PA
401-331-5810	Providence*	RI
423-974-9200	Knoxville*	TN
512-472-4931	Austin	TX
214-363-9941	Dallas	TX

Council Travel (cont'd)		713-743-2777	Houston	TX	
		801-375-1919	Provo	UT	
		801-582-5840	Salt Lake City	UT	
		206-632-2448	Seattle*	WA	
		206-329-4567	Seattle*	WA	
		608-280-8906	Madison	WI	

www.counciltravel.com
Worldwide student travel. More locations on web site.
*These offices sell RTW tickets.

Council Wholesale	800-347-2433	212-822-2800	New York	NY	T

Worldwide, Student fares

Crown Peters Travel	800-321-1199	718-932-7800	Astoria	NY	B

Europe, Middle East, Cairo, Istanbul

CTI Carriers	800-363-8181	416-429-9000	Toronto	ON	T

Europe (fr. Canada), Egypt, Turkey, hotels & tours

Custom Travel	800-535-9797	415-239-4200	Daly City	CA	B

Worldwide, charters, tours, wholesales for Aeroflot

Cut Rate Travel	800-388-0575	847-405-0575	Deerfield	IL	B

www.cutratetravel.xt.com
Worldwide (exc. Canada)

Cut-Throat Travel		415-989-8747	San Francisco	CA	P

Worldwide

CWT Vacations	800-223-6862	212-695-8435	New York	NY	B

Worldwide, US, last-minute tickets, flexible fares

D-FW Tours	800-527-2589	972-980-4540	Dallas	TX	B

www.dfwtours.com
Worldwide (exc. Caribbean, Hawaii), US

Dan Travel	800-362-1308	301-907-8977	Bethesda	MD	B

www.dantravel.com
C. & S. America

Delights Travel		604-876-8278	Vancouver	BC	T

Asia, packages for Chinese speakers

Democracy Travel	800-536-8728	202-965-7200	Washington	DC	B

RTW, Circle Pacific, Worldwide, hotels

DER Travel Services	800-717-4247	847-430-0000	Rosemont	IL	B

www.dertravel.com
Worldwide, special arrangement with Lufthansa

Detours	800-252-8780	516-763-1900	Oceanside	NY	B

Worldwide

Dial Europe		212-758-5310	New York	NY	B

Worldwide, specializes in 1st & Business class

Dial Europe		212-758-5310	New York	NY	B
	Worldwide, specializes in 1st & Business class				
Diplomat Tours	800-727-8687	916-972-1500	Sacramento	CA	T
	Worldwide				
Discount Tickets	888-382-4327	212-391-2313	New York	NY	B
	US, last minute				
Discount Travel		310-641-5343	Santa Clarita	CA	P
	Europe, charters				
Discount Travel	888-738-8747	504-761-4711	Baton Rouge	LA	P
	Worldwide, Las Vegas, US				
Discover Africa	888-330-4880	216-595-9775	Beachwood	OH	B
	Africa				
Discover Wholesale Travel	800-576-7770	949-833-1136	Irvine	CA	P
	Europe, Asia, S. Pacific				
Dloomy World Travel	800-356-6697	310-358-1400	Beverly Hills	CA	B
	Europe, Africa, Middle East				
Dollar Saver Travel		913-381-5050	Overland Park	KS	P
	www.dstravel.com				
	Worldwide, India				
Downtown Travel	800-952-3519	212-766-5705	New York	NY	B
	Europe, Asia (Aeroflot, Finnair)				
DownUnder Direct	800-642-6224	610-896-1741	Ardmore	PA	B
	www.swainaustralia.com				
	Australia, S. Pacific				
Earth Travel	800-203-1518	212-594-3553	New York	NY	B
	Asia				
Eastern Europe Tours	800-441-1339	206-448-8400	Seattle	WA	B
	www.imp-world-tours.com				
	Europe (Eastern), S. America, SAS, LAN Chile				
Economy Travel	888-222-2110	770-290-7730	Atlanta	GA	P
	www.economytravel.com				
	Worldwide, US				
Egypt National Tours & Travel	877-993-4978	702-696-0084	Las Vegas	NV	T
	Worldwide, US				
Egypt Tours & Travel	800-523-4978	773-506-9999	Chicago	IL	B
	www.egypttours.com				
	Middle East (Egypt, Israel)				
Elite Tours & Travel	800-354-8320	216-514-9000	Woodmere	OH	B
	Middle East				

Embassy Tours	800-299-5284	972-985-2929	Plano	TX	B
	www.embassytravel.com				
	C. & S. America				
EST International Travel		713-974-0521	Houston	TX	B
	Worldwide, charters, packages				
EuroGroups	800-462-2577	914-682-7456	White Plains	NY	B
	www.eurogroups.com				
	Europe, groups of 10+ only				
Europak Scan Div.	800-253-1342		Baltimore	MD	T
	Europe				
Europe On Line	800-587-4849	941-263-3937	Naples	FL	B
	Europe (Germany fr. Florida)				
European Tours	800-882-3983	213-624-9378	Los Angeles	CA	B
	www.europtours.com				
	Europe				
Everest Travel		770-220-1866	Atlanta	GA	T
	www.everesttravel.com				
	Worldwide				
EZ Travel		206-524-1977	Seattle	WA	B
	Middle East, Worldwide, US (Las Vegas)				
F.O.S. Tours	800-367-3450	516-466-5651	Great Neck	NY	B
	www.fostours.com				
	Europe (Eastern)				
Falcon Travel & Tours	800-272-6394	718-522-0692	Brooklyn	NY	B
	Worldwide				
Fana Travels	800-600-3262	202-667-0101	Washington	DC	B
	Europe, Africa, Middle East, India, US				
Fantasy Holidays	800-645-2555	516-935-8500	Jericho	NY	T
	www.fantasyholidays.com				
	Europe, Italy, Hawaii				
Fare Deal Travel	800-243-2785	619-282-8866	San Diego	CA	P
	www.faredealtravel.com				
	Europe, US				
Fare Deals Ltd.	800-347-7006	410-581-8787	Owings Mills	MD	P
	www.faredeal.com				
	Caribbean, US, Hawaii, Worldwide, charters				
Fare Deals Travel	800-878-2929	303-792-2929	Englewood	CO	P
	www.faredealstravel.com				
	Worldwide, US				

Fare Game		941-430-1440	Naples	FL	T
	www.escope.com				
	Worldwide				
Favored Holidays		718-934-8881	Brooklyn	NY	B
	Europe				
Fellowship Travel International	800-446-7667	804-264-0121	Richmond	VA	B
	www.fellowship.com				
	Worldwide, missionary travel				
Ferns Travel	800-790-1016	212-868-9194	New York	NY	B
	Europe (Scandinavia), S. America				
Festival of Asia	800-533-9953	415-908-6980	San Francisco	CA	B
	www.asiafest.com				
	Asia, Australia				
First Discount Travel	800-951-9558	501-219-1893	Little Rock	AR	P
	www.1stdisctravel.com				
	Worldwide				
First Discount Travel	888-819-4646	503-848-4646	Aloha	OR	P
	www.1discount-travel.com				
	Worldwide				
Flight Coordinators	800-544-3644	310-581-5600	Santa Monica	CA	P
	Worldwide				
Fly Wise Travel	800-347-3939	212-869-2223	New York	NY	B
	www.checkairfare.com				
	US, Worldwide, last minute				
Flytime Tour & Travel	800-786-4388	212-760-3737	New York	NY	B
	Europe, Asia				
Foreign Indep. Tours	800-248-3487	201-585-1549	Fort Lee	NJ	B
	www.fitnile.com				
	Middle East (Egypt), Africa (Kenya)				
Four Seasons Travel		604-263-9915	Vancouver	BC	P
	Asia				
Frosch Int'l Travel	800-866-1623	713-850-1556	Houston	TX	B
	www.froschtravel.com				
	S. Africa, Middle East (Israel), hotels				
G A 2000	888-422-2216	212-903-3538	New York	NY	T
	Europe, Italy, Middle East, Africa				
G. G. Tours	800-504-5557	416-487-1146	Toronto	ON	T
	www.ggtours.on.ca				
	Trinidad, Caribbean				

Gama Tours	800-747-7235	201-662-1000	N. Bergen	NJ	B
	www.israelplus.com				
	Europe, Middle East, Israel				
Garden State Travel		201-333-1232	Jersey City	NJ	B
	www.gardenstatetravel.com				
	Asia, Manila				
Gary Marcus Travel	800-524-0821	973-731-7600	West Orange	NJ	B
	US (Las Vegas), Caribbean, Aruba				
Gate 1	800-682-3333	215-572-7676	Glenside	PA	T
	www.gate1travel.com				
	Europe, Middle East, Israel, Mediterranean, Asia (China), India, Africa, El Al, TWA, Catholic pilgrimages				
General Tours	800-221-2216		Keene	NH	T
	www.generaltours.com				
	Europe, Middle East, India, C. & S. America				
Gerosa Tours	800-243-7672	703-415-4795	Arlington	VA	B
	S. America, Europe				
Getaway Travel	800-683-6336	305-446-7855	Coral Gables	FL	T
	www.getawaytravel.com				
	C. & S. America, Europe, Asia				
Ghana America Vacations	888-774-4262	202-862-4959	Washington	DC	B
	www.intraworld-exchange.com				
	Africa				
Glavs Travel	800-336-5727	212-290-3300	New York	NY	B
	www.glavs.com				
	Europe, Asia (Russia & CIS), Aeroflot, Trans Air				
Global Adventures Travel	800-989-6017	925-689-8883	Concord	CA	P
	www.globaladv.com				
	Worldwide, RTW, Circle Pacific				
Global Discount Travel Services	800-497-6678		Las Vegas	NV	P
	www.lowestfare.com				
	US				
Global Journeys	888-743-6999	212-221-0710	New York	NY	B
	www.get-travel.com				
	Middle East				
Global Travel Consolidator	800-366-3544	310-581-5610	Santa Monica	CA	T
	Worldwide (exc. Australia & S. Pacific)				
Globe Travel Specialist	800-969-4562	212-843-9885	New York	NY	B
	Europe, Asia, S. America, hotels				

Globe Travels		319-362-9071	Cedar Rapids	IA	P
	www.globetravels.com				
	Europe, Asia, India				
Go Away Travel	800-387-8850	416-322-1034	Toronto	ON	T
	Australia, N. Zealand, S. Pacific, Asia, Southern Africa				
Golden Tour	877-455-6888	770-455-8686	Atlanta	GA	T
	Asia				
Great Tours	800-607-7066	651-439-0690	Stillwater	MN	T
	Europe (Eastern), CIS (Czech Air, Malev, Austrian, Moldova Airlines)				
Group & Leisure Travel	800-874-6608	816-690-4040	Oak Grove	MO	P
	Worldwide, US on TWA (exc. to & fr. St. Louis)				
GTI Travel Consolidators	800-829-8234	616-396-1234	Holland	MI	B
	Europe, Eastern Europe, Asia				
GTT International	800-878-4283	972-960-2000	Dallas	TX	T
	Worldwide, US				
Guardian Travel Service	800-741-3050	727-585-3322	Largo	FL	T
	Europe, UK, Middle East (Israel)				
Hana Travel	800-962-8044	847-913-1177	Buffalo Grove	IL	B
	Asia, hotels				
Hans World Travel	800-421-4267	301-770-1717	Rockville	MD	B
	www.hanstravel.com				
	Europe, Asia				
Happy Tours Vacations	800-877-4277	408-461-0013	Scotts Valley	CA	T
	Hawaii, S. Pacific (Fiji, Tahiti, Cook Islands) C. America (Baja Mexico)				
Hari World Travel		404-233-5005	Atlanta	GA	B
		773-381-5555	Chicago	IL	
		212-957-3000	New York	NY	
	www.hariworld.com				
	India, Europe, US				
High Adventure	800-350-0612	415-912-5600	San Francisco	CA	B
	www.highadv.com				
	RTW, adventure travel				
Hillcrest Tours	800-268-3820	905-884-1832	Richmond Hill	ON	T
	US, Europe, Caribbean (US Airways)				
Himalayan Int'l Tours		212-564-5164	New York	NY	B
	www.himalayantours.com				
	Asia, India, Tibet				
Holiday Tours	800-393-1212	626-795-1012	Pasadena	CA	B
	C. & S. America				

Holiday Travel International	800-775-7111	724-863-7500	N. Huntingdon	PA	B
	www.holidaytvl.com				
	US, Las Vegas, Reno				
Homeric Tours & Charters	800-223-5570	212-753-1100	New York	NY	B
	www.homerictours.com				
	Europe (Greece, Portugal), Africa (Morocco), Middle East (Egypt)				
Hostways Travel	800-327-3207	954-966-8500	Ft. Lauderdale	FL	B
	Worldwide, cruises				
Hot Spot Tours	800-433-0075	212-421-9090	New York	NY	T
	Charters to Caribbean				
HTI Tours	800-441-4411	215-563-8484	Philadelphia	PA	T
	Worldwide, one-ways				
Hungarian Travel	800-624-9277	818-996-3510	Receda	CA	T
	www.hungariantravel.com				
	Europe (Hungary, Eastern Europe, Vienna), some US				
Inclusive Holidays	800-238-2140	203-454-2233	Westport	CT	B
	Caribbean, Europe				
Inka's Empire Tours		212-875-0370	New York	NY	B
	www.inkas.com				
	S. America (Peru, Bolivia)				
Inta-Aussie Tours	800-531-9222	310-568-2060	Los Angeles	CA	T
	www.inta-aussie.com				
	Australia, New Zealand, S. Pacific				
Intair Transit		514-286-7078	Montreal	PQ	T
	www.intairtransit.qc.ca				
	Worldwide, US, 63 airlines				
Integrity Travel	800-468-4272	406-755-8484	Kalispell	MT	P
	Worldwide				
Inter-Island Tours	800-245-3434	212-686-4868	New York	NY	T
	www.interislandtours.com				
	Caribbean				
International Disc't Travel	800-466-7357	703-750-0101	Alexandria	VA	B
	Europe, S. America, Australia, New Zealand				
International Travel Exchange	800-727-7830	212-808-5368	New York	NY	B
	www.flyite.com				
	US, Europe, Africa, Middle East				
International Travel Systems	800-258-0135	201-727-0470	Hasbr'ck Hgts	NJ	T
	www.etravelbid.com				
	Asia, Middle East, Australia, N. Zealand, 1st & Business class to Europe				

International Ventures	800-727-5475	203-761-1110	Wilton	CT	B
	www.internationalventures.com				
	S. Africa				
Intervac	800-992-9629	305-670-8990	Miami	FL	T
	www.intervac.com				
	Caribbean				
Interworld Travel	800-468-3796	305-443-4929	Coral Gables	FL	B
	www.interworldtravel.com				
	Europe, UK, S. Africa, S. America fr. New York				
Intourist USA	800-556-530	561-585-5305	Lake Worth	FL	B
	www.intourist.ru				
	Europe (Finland, Russia), Asia (China, Mongolia)				
Intratours	800-334-8069	713-952-0662	Houston	TX	T
	Europe (Spain), C. & S. America				
Ireland-UK Consolidated	888-577-2900	212-661-1999	New York	NY	T
	www.irelandair.com				
	Europe (Ireland, UK)				
Isram World of Travel	800-223-7460	212-983-8381	New York	NY	T
	www.isram.com				
	Middle East (Israel, Jordan)				
Italiatour	800-237-0517	212-903-3300	New York	NY	T
	www.italiatour.com				
	Europe (Italy)				
ITS Tours & Travel	800-533-8688	409-764-0518	College Station	TX	B
	www.sightseeing.com/moscow.htm				
	Europe (Eastern, Russia), Asia (CIS), India				
J & O Air	800-877-8111	619-282-4124	San Diego	CA	T
	Worldwide (30 airlines)				
Jade Tours	800-561-5233	604-689-5885	Vancouver	BC	T
	S.E. Asia (15 airlines), US				
Japan Express		213-680-0550	Los Angeles	CA	B
	Asia (Japan)				
Japan Travel Service	800-822-3336	770-451-3607	Atlanta	GA	B
	Japan, Asia				
Jaya Travel	877-359-5292	312-606-9600	Chicago	IL	P
		248-372-4800	Southfield	MI	
		212-697-0022	New York	NY	
	www.jayatravel.com				
	Worldwide, US				
Jensen Baron	800-333-2060	801-267-5757	Salt Lake City	UT	B
	Worldwide				

Jetset Tours Inc.	800-638-3273	323-290-5800	Los Angeles	CA	T
		619-542-1602	San Diego	CA	
		415-546-1204	San Francisco	CA	
		352-394-3370	Clermont	FL	
		312-362-9779	Chicago	IL	
		212-818-9756	New York	NY	
		713-961-0080	Houston	TX	
		206-623-6388	Seattle	WA	

www.jetset.com
Worldwide, some US (LA, NY, Chicago), Hawaii

Jetway Tours	800-421-8771	818-990-2918	Los Angeles	CA	B

Europe, S. America, S.E. Asia, hotels in Asia

K&K Travel	800-523-1374	714-448-9678	Fullerton	CA	P

Europe, Asia, S. Pacific

Kambi Travel International	800-220-2192	301-925-9012	Landover	MD	B

Europe, Asia, Africa (W. Africa)

Karell Travel	800-327-0373	305-446-7766	Coral Gables	FL	B

www.karell.com
S. Africa

Katy Van Tours	800-808-8747	281-492-7032	Houston	TX	B

Europe, Asia, S. America, Middle East

King Tut Tours, Inc.	800-398-1888	510-791-2907	Fremont	CA	B

www.kingtuttours.com
Worldwide

Kristensen Int'l Travel & Tours	800-262-8728	612-854-5589	Bloomington	MN	P

www.kitt-travel.com
S. Pacific, Australia, N. Zealand

KTS Services	800-531-6677	718-454-2300	Jamaica	NY	B

Europe, Germany

Kutrubes Travel	800-878-8566	617-426-5668	Boston	MA	B

www.kutrubestravel.com
Europe (Greece, Albania), Middle East (Lebanon)

L. T. & Travel	800-295-3436	212-682-2748	New York	NY	B

Caribbean, US, Hawaii

Latin Adventure Tours	888-293-0780	407-339-9296	Longwood	FL	B

C. & S. America, Caribbean

Latin American Travel	800-252-0775	713-774-0600	Houston	TX	B

www.latinamericantravel.com
C. & S. America, Caribbean (Jamaica)

Le Soleil Tours	800-225-4723	212-687-2600	New York	NY	B

Europe (France, Spain), Africa (Morocco)

Levon Travel	800-445-3866	323-871-8711	Los Angeles	CA	B
	www.levontravel.com				
	Europe, Middle East, Armenia, US				
Lomantours & Travel Service	800-344-8054	305-573-4011	Miami	FL	T
	C. & S. America				
Lotus International Tours	800-450-4638	714-892-8502	Westminster	CA	B
	www.lotustravel.com				
	Middle East				
Magical Holidays	800-433-7773	415-781-1345	San Francisco	CA	T
	Africa				
Magical Holidays	800-235-4225	704-357-1820	Charlotte	NC	B
	800-228-2208	212-486-9600	New York	NY	
	Africa, Europe				
Malaysia Travel Advisors	800-359-8655	618-351-9398	Carbondale	IL	B
	www.mta-tvl.com				
	S.E. Asia (Malaysia)				
Marakesh Tourist Company	800-458-1772	201-435-2800	Jersey City	NJ	B
	www.marakeshtouristco.com				
	Europe, Middle East				
Marco Polo	800-831-3108	206-621-0700	Seattle	WA	T
	Asia				
McAbee Tours	800-622-2335	770-396-9988	Atlanta	GA	T
	www.mcabee.com				
	Worldwide				
Mena Tours & Travel	800-937-6362	773-275-2125	Chicago	IL	B
	www.menatours.net				
	C. & S. America, Caribbean				
Mercury Tours & Travel	877-711-8687	212-268-7434	New York	NY	B
	US				
Middle East Travel Center	800-672-0514	214-637-0514	Dallas	TX	T
	800-444-2995	713-952-3904	Houston	TX	
	Middle East, Africa, Asia, Europe				
Midtown Travel Consultants	800-548-8904	404-872-8308	Atlanta	GA	B
	Worldwide				
Mile High Tours	800-777-8687	303-758-8246	Denver	CO	B
	US, Las Vegas, C. America (Mexico)				
Mill-Run Tours	800-645-5786		Miami	FL	T
		312-641-5914	Chicago	IL	
		201-894-1200	Englew'd Cliffs	NJ	
		212-486-9840	New York	NY	
		713-961-3666	Houston	TX	
	Worldwide				

Mirabel Travel	800-890-4590	305-937-4880	Miami Beach	FL	B
	Europe, Middle East (Israel)				
MLT Vacations	800-328-0025	612-672-3111	Minnetonka	MN	T
	US, Caribbean, C. America (Mexico)				
Moment's Notice		212-486-0500	New York	NY	P
	www.moments-notice.com				
	Worldwide, Hawaii, US (Las Vegas, Disney)				
Monica Travel &		301-294-1166	Rockville	MD	B
Tours	Europe, Africa, Middle East, C. & S. America				
Mr. Cheap's		212-431-1616	New York	NY	P
	US, Worldwide (exc. S. America & Africa)				
Mr. Cheap's Travel	800-672-4327	303-758-3833	Denver	CO	P
		503-557-9101	Clackamas	OR	
	www.mrcheaps.com				
	US, Europe, last minute				
National Travel	800-228-6886	312-939-2190	Chicago	IL	P
Centre	Asia, S. Pacific				
Natrabu Indonesian	800-628-7228	415-362-4225	San Francisco	CA	B
Travel & Tours	www.travelfile.com/get/natrabu				
	S.E. Asia				
Nefertai Travel	888-616-3337	212-697-5563	New York	NY	B
	www.nefertai.com				
	Europe, Middle East, US				
New Europe	800-642-3874	212-686-2424	New York	NY	B
Holidays	Europe, Middle East, Asia				
New Frontiers USA	800-366-6387	212-779-0600	New York	NY	B
	www.newfrontiers.com				
	Europe, England, France, Italy, charters to Paris				
New Frontiers	800-677-0720	310-670-7318	Los Angeles	CA	B
West	www.newfrontiers.com				
	Europe, England, France, Italy, charters to Paris				
New Wave Travel	800-220-9283	206-527-3579	Seattle	WA	B
	Asia				
North Star Tours	800-431-1511	954-776-7070	Ft. Lauderdale	FL	B
	www.passagetours.com				
	Europe (Scandinavia)				
Northwest World	800-800-1504		Minnetonka	MN	P
Vacations	800-727-1111	612-470-1111	Minnetonka	MN	T
	Europe, Asia, India, Caribbean, US/Canada,				
	C. America (Mexico)				

Nova Travel	800-334-1188	503-697-4460	Portland	OR	B
	www.novatravel.com				
	Asia, India, US				
Number One Travel	800-475-1009	813-872-6900	Tampa	FL	B
	home.att.net/~onetravel				
	Asia, China, Korea				
O'Connor Fairways Travel	800-662-0550	212-661-0550	New York	NY	P
	www.oconnors.com				
	Europe (Ireland, UK)				
Odyssey Travel		613-549-3553	Kingston	ON	P
		613-789-1900	Ottawa	ON	
	www.odyssey-travel.com				
	Worldwide, RTW, Circle Pacific, US				
Online Travel	800-660-5300	847-318-8890	Rosemont	IL	P
	www.eurorail.com				
	Europe, Middle East, C. & S. America, rail passes				
Orbis Polish Travel	800-867-6526	212-867-5011	New York	NY	B
	www.orbis-usa.com				
	Europe (Poland, Eastern), hotels, cars				
Overseas Express	800-343-4873	773-262-4971	Chicago	IL	B
	800-750-1224	972-819-2000	Irving	TX	
	www.ovex.com				
	Europe, Africa, Middle East, Asia				
Overseas Travel	800-783-7196	303-337-7196	Aurora	CO	B
	Europe, Middle East, Africa, Asia, S. America				
Oxford Travel	800-851-5290	914-838-1122	Beacon	NY	B
	Europe, Africa, S. America, Asia				
P&F International	800-444-6666	718-937-1998	Astoria	NY	B
	Europe, Middle East, C. & S. America				
Pacesetter Travel	800-663-5115	604-687-3083	Vancouver	BC	P
	S. Pacific, Africa, Asia				
Pacific Gateway	800-777-8369	503-294-6478	Portland	OR	T
		206-624-2228	Seattle	WA	
	Worldwide, US				
Pacific Holidays	800-355-8025	212-764-1977	New York	NY	B
	www.travelfile.com/get/pacifhol.htm				
	Asia				
Pali Tours & Travel		808-533-3608	Honolulu	HI	B
	Worldwide				
Palm Coast Travel	800-444-1560	561-733-9950	Boynton Bch	FL	B
	Europe (Scandinavia), Asia, S. America				

Palmair	800-526-5892	415-826-8990	San Francisco	CA	B
	www.palmairinternational.com				
	Europe, Africa, Middle East				
Panda Travel	800-447-2632	602-943-3383	Phoenix	AZ	P
	www.pandatravel.com				
	Worldwide, US, cruises				
Panorama Travel	800-204-7130	212-741-0033	New York	NY	B
	www.panoramatravel.com				
	Europe (Eastern & Russia), Asia (Central)				
Panorama World Tours & Travel	800-475-9339	216-228-9339	Lakewood	OH	B
	www.panoramaholidays.com				
	Europe, Asia, Middle East, S. Pacific				
Passport Travel Management	800-950-5864	813-931-3166	Tampa	FL	B
	Asia, S. Pacific				
Paul Laifer Tours	800-346-6314	973-887-1188	Parsippany	NJ	B
	www.laifertours.com				
	Europe (Eastern), hotels				
Payless Travel	800-892-0027	212-573-8986	New York	NY	B
	www.pltravel.com				
	Europe, Africa, Australia, US				
PCS Travel		213-239-2424	Los Angeles	CA	T
	Asia, Japan				
PCS Travel		213-239-2440	Los Angeles	CA	B
		415-972-8101	San Francisco	CA	
		202-833-3531	Washington	DC	
		206-682-8350	Seattle	WA	
	Asia, Japan				
Pennsylvania Travel	800-331-0947	610-251-9944	Paoli	PA	P
	www.patravel.com				
	Worldwide, US				
Perfect Travel	800-352-5359	516-791-9089	Cedarhurst	NY	B
	www.1800elalfly.com				
	Middle East (Israel)				
PERS Travel Inc.	800-583-0909	202-338-2121	Washington	DC	B
	Middle East (Iran)				
Persvoyage	888-455-7377	561-347-0900	Boca Raton	FL	B
	Europe, Middle East, Teheran				
Peru Unlimited	800-947-5655	212-995-9786	New York	NY	B
	S. America (Peru, Chile, Bolivia, Argentina)				
Pharos Travel & Tourism	877-999-5511	212-736-6070	New York	NY	B
	Middle East, Europe, US				

Picasso Travel	800-742-2776	310-645-4400	Los Angeles	CA	T
		650-579-1900	San Francisco	CA	
		312-580-1000	Chicago	IL	
		617-859-5832	Boston	MA	
		212-244-5454	New York	NY	
	Worldwide				
Pino Welcome Travel	800-247-6578	212-682-5400	New York	NY	B
	www.pinotravel.com				
	Europe (Italy), S. America, Asia, Africa, US				
Pinto Basto USA	800-526-8539	914-639-8020	New City	NY	B
	www.pousada.com				
	Europe (Portugal, Spain), C. America (Costa Rica)				
Pioneer Tours	800-288-2107	408-648-8800	Monterey	CA	T
	C. & S. America				
Pleasure Break Vacations	800-777-1566	414-934-1882	Milwaukee	WI	B
	www.pleasurebreak.com				
	Europe (Ireland & Eastern), Africa, Middle East, C. America (Costa Rica, Belize)				
Plus Ultra Tours	800-242-0394	718-278-1818	Astoria	NY	T
	www.spaintours.com				
	Europe (Spain, Portugal), Africa (Morocco)				
Premier Travel Services Inc.	800-545-1910	215-893-9966	Philadelphia	PA	B
	www.premiertours.com				
	Southern Africa				
Prestige Tour & Travel	800-232-9638	212-779-8371	New York	NY	B
	www.prestigetour.com				
	Africa				
Prime Travel	800-344-3962	201-825-1600	Ramsey	NJ	B
	www.primetravel.com				
	Europe, Middle East, Asia, CIS				
Prime Travel Services	800-447-4013	305-441-0622	Coral Gables	FL	T
	C. & S. America				
Professional Travel Service	800-289-0549	323-852-0549	Beverly Hills	CA	B
	www.pro-travel.com				
	S. America				
Queue Travel	800-356-4871	305-445-7740	Coral Gables	FL	B
	Europe, S. & C. America, Russia				
Rahway Travel	800-526-2786	732-381-8800	Rahway	NJ	B
	Europe (Eastern & Ukraine)				
Raj Travels	888-359-4685	212-697-4612	New York	NY	B
	India, Asia, Europe				

Raptim Travel	800-777-9232	716-754-9232	Lewiston	NY	B
	Worldwide (religious travel)				
Rebel Tours & Travel	800-227-3235	661-294-0900	Valencia	CA	B
	www.rebeltours.com				
	Western Europe, Holland				
Red Star Travel	800-215-4378		Seattle	WA	P
	www.irkutsk-baikal.com				
	Europe (CIS), Asia (CIS)				
Regatta Travel	800-445-7685	303-751-0666	Aurora	CO	P
	Worldwide via Denver, US				
Regent Travel Network		404-248-8062	Atlanta	GA	B
	www.rcna.com				
	Asia				
Reko Tours	800-536-1866	718-932-3232	Astoria	NY	T
	www.aegeanholidays.com				
	Worldwide				
Riverside Travel		808-521-5645	Honolulu	HI	P
	Worldwide				
Rockwell Tours	800-526-4910	831-461-0133	Scotts Valley	CA	B
	www.happytours.com				
	Caribbean, C. America (Mexico)				
Royal Lane Travel	800-329-2030	214-340-2030	Dallas	TX	B
	Worldwide				
RTS Travel Services	800-853-1128	850-243-2662	Ft. Walton Bch	FL	P
	www.yourvacation.com				
	Worldwide				
Rupa Travel Service		732-572-5000	Edison	NJ	B
	www.rupatravels.com				
	Worldwide, US				
Russart Travel	888-338-7877	415-781-6655	San Francisco	CA	P
	Europe, Russia				
Sae Han Travel & Tours	800-421-5489	213-383-4988	Los Angeles	CA	B
	Asia				
SAF Travel World	800-394-8587	609-216-2900	Cherry Hill	NJ	B
		215-440-7600	Philadelphia	PA	
	Asia (Philippines, Vietnam), Europe, US				
Safariline	877-723-2745	847-914-9300	Lincolnshire	IL	B
	www.safarilinetravel.com				
	Africa, Mediterranean, Spain, Turkey				

Scan The World		650-325-0876	Palo Alto	CA B
www.scantheworld.com				
Europe, Africa, Australia, RTW, US				
Sceptre Tours & Charters	800-221-0924	516-255-9800	Rockville Ctr	NY B
www.sceptretours.com				
Ireland				
Seamorgh Travel	800-543-2994	973-376-1141	Millburn	NJ B
Worldwide (exc. Asia)				
Senator Travel	800-736-2121	323-782-9500	Beverly Hills	CA B
www.senatortravel.com				
Europe, 1st & Business class				
Sharp Travel	800-220-2165	301-731-3355	Landover	MD B
Worldwide (exc. Asia), US				
Sharp Travel Agency	800-969-7427	703-941-2929	Annandale	VA B
Asia, India, US				
Sharp Travel Headquarters	800-252-1170	212-465-9500	New York	NY B
www.sharp-travel.com				
S.E. Asia				
SITA World Travel		818-767-0039	Sun Valley	CA P
Africa, Asia, India				
Sky Bird Travel & Tours	887-759-2473	312-606-9600	Chicago	IL T
	887-759-2473	248-372-4800	Southfield	MI
	887-759-2473	212-697-0022	New York	NY
www.skybird-travel.com				
Worldwide, US, cruises				
Skylink Travel	800-247-6659	213-653-6718	Los Angeles	CA T
		202-822-6666	Washington	DC
		312-263-7664	Chicago	IL
		212-573-8980	New York	NY
Europe, Middle East, Africa; Asia fr. NY office				
Skytours Travel	800-246-8687	415-228-8228	San Francisco	CA B
www.skytours.com				
Europe (Scandinavia & Eastern), S. America, Asia				
Skyway Travel		404-252-2152	Atlanta	GA B
Asia, Europe, Middle East, Africa				
Solar Tours	800-388-7652	202-861-5864	Washington	DC T
	800-727-7652	941-966-1664	Sarasota	FL
www.solartours.com				
Europe, C. & S. America				
Sona Travels	800-720-7662	301-589-3344	Silver Spring	MD B
	800-721-7662	703-528-6644	Arlington	VA
Europe, Middle East, S. America (Bolivia), India, US				

South American Fiesta	800-334-3782 770-321-6814 Atlanta www.southamericanfiesta.com C. & S. America, hotels		GA	B
South Pacific Express Travel	800-321-7739 415-982-6833 San Francisco www.1stoptravel.com S. Pacific, Asia, Europe, US		CA	B
South Star Tours	800-654-4468 310-416-1001 El Segundo www.travelx.com/sostar.htm C. & S. America, educational tours		CA	B
Southern Connections	800-635-3303 818-508-8899 N. Hollywood C. & S. America		CA	P
Southwest Travel Systems	800-314-6111 602-952-6900 Phoenix www.swtravel.com Europe fr. Phoenix, S.E. Asia, S. America, S. Pacific packages		AZ	T
Spanish Heritage Tours	800-221-2580 718-544-2752 Forest Hills www.shtours.com Europe (Spain & Portugal)		NY	B
Spector Travel	800-879-2374 617-338-0111 Boston www.spectortravel.com Africa		MA	B
STA Travel	800-781-4040			P
	800-777-0112	(nat'l res. ctr.) Scottsdale	AZ	
		602-921-1988 Tempe	AZ	
		510-642-3000 Berkeley	CA	
		323-934-8722 Los Angeles	CA	
		310-824-1574 Los Angeles	CA	
	800-925-4777	(groups) Los Angeles	CA	
		619-270-1750 San Diego	CA	
		415-391-8407 San Francisco	CA	
		310-394-5126 Santa Monica	CA	
		202-877-0912 Washington	DC	
		305-284-1044 Coral Gables	FL	
		352-338-0068 Gainesville	FL	
		407-541-2000 Orlando	FL	
		813-974-3380 Tampa	FL	
		312-786-9050 Chicago	IL	
		504-334-2516 Baton Rouge	LA	
		617-373-7900 Boston	MA	
		617-266-6014 Boston	MA	
		617-576-4623 Cambridge	MA	
		734-968-5151 Ann Arbor	MI	
		612-615-1800 Minneapolis	MN	

STA Travel (cont'd)	212-627-3111	New York	NY	
	212-865-2700	New York	NY	
	215-568-7999	Philadelphia	PA	
	512-472-2900	Austin	TX	
	804-924-4445	Charlottesville	VA	
	206-633-5000	Seattle	WA	
	608-263-8810	Madison	WI	

www.sta-travel.com
Worldwide student travel. International offices are listed on the web site.

STT Worldwide Travel 800-975-1995 213-655-8866 Los Angeles CA T
800-655-8866 503-641-8866 Beaverton OR
Asia, Europe, US

Student Travel Services 800-648-4849 410-859-4200 Hanover MD B
Caribbean

Sun Destination Travel 415-398-1313 San Francisco CA P
www.enterit.net/Sun1313
Worldwide, US

Sun Island Holidays 800-824-4653 516-364-4000 Syosset NY T
Caribbean

Sunny Land Tours 800-783-7839 201-487-2150 Hackensack NJ B
www.sunnylandtours.com
Worldwide, adventure travel

Sunrise Tours 800-872-3801 212-947-3617 New York NY T
Europe (Eastern, Baltic, Russia), Middle East, Asia

Suntrips 800-786-8747 408-432-1101 San Jose CA B
Hawaii, C. America (Mexico), Europe (Portugal, the Azores)

Super Travel & Tours 800-878-7371 212-986-8002 New York NY B
Pakistan

Supersonic Travel 323-851-0333 Hollywood CA B
Worldwide, US, hotels

Swain Australia Tours 800-227-9246 610-896-9595 Ardmore PA B
www.swaintours.com
Australia, New Zealand, S. Pacific

TAL Tours 800-825-9399 516-825-0966 Valley Stream NY T
www.taltours.com
Middle East (Israel)

TCI Travel 800-333-7033 214-630-3344 Dallas TX B
Europe, Middle East, Africa

TFI Tours Int'l 800-745-8000 212-736-1140 New York NY B
Worldwide, US, S. America, Europe, 61 airlines

The Africa Desk	800-284-8796	860-354-9341	New Milford	CT	B
	www.africadesk.com				
	Africa				
The Budget Traveler		415-331-3700	Sausalito	CA	B
	Europe, C. America				
The Egyptian Connection	800-334-4477	718-380-4330	Fresh Meadws	NY	B
	www.egyptontheweb.com				
	Israel, Middle East, Africa, Europe (France)				
The French Experience		212-986-3800	New York	NY	P
	www.frenchexperience.com				
	Europe (France); the name says it all				
The Last Minute Club	800-563-2582	416-441-2582	North York	ON	P
	www.lastminuteclub.com				
	Worldwide, US, Canada				
Ticket Planet	800-799-8888	415-288-9999	San Francisco	CA	B
	www.ticketplanet.com				
	Worldwide, RTW, Circle Pacific, 1st & Business class				
Time Travel	800-847-7026	630-595-8463	Bensenville	IL	T
	Europe, Asia				
TMV Tours		404-256-4809	Atlanta	GA	B
		773-785-6400	Chicago	IL	
		617-426-6181	Boston	MA	
		908-603-8484	Edison	NJ	
		201-656-6650	Jersey City	NJ	
	www.tmvtours.com				
	Middle East, Asia, Africa, India				
Tokyo Travel Service	800-227-2065	213-680-3545	Los Angeles	CA	B
	Asia, some Europe & S. America				
Tourlite Int'l	800-272-7600	212-599-2727	New York	NY	B
	www.tourlite.com				
	Mediterranean, S. & C. America				
Tours International	800-247-7965	713-223-5544	Houston	TX	B
	www.toursinternational.com				
	S. America				
Trade Wind Associates	800-268-4853	604-683-6900	Vancouver	BC	B
	800-438-4853	312-664-3434	Chicago	IL	
	800-438-4853	212-286-0667	New York	NY	
	800-268-4853	416-966-4853	Toronto	ON	
	800-438-4853	713-960-0343	Houston	TX	
	www.twai.com				
	Worldwide, US				

Tradesco Tours	800-833-3402	310-649-5808	Los Angeles	CA	B
	www.tradescotours.com				
	Europe (Eastern)				
Trans Am Travel	800-600-1567	310-670-2111	Los Angeles	CA	T
		415-397-1122	San Francisco	CA	
	800-822-7600	312-214-4411	Chicago	IL	
		212-730-4980	New York	NY	
	800-600-1548	703-998-7676	Alexandria	VA	
	www.transamtravel.com				
	Worldwide				
Transview Travel	800-553-6762	703-912-3900	Burke	VA	B
	Worldwide, Pakistan, India				
Travac Tours & Charters	800-872-8800	407-896-0014	Orlando	FL	B
		212-563-3303	New York	NY	
	www.thetravelsite.com (P)				
	www.travac.com (T)				
	Europe, some Middle East, Africa, Asia & C. & S America				
Travel Abroad	800-297-8788	212-564-8989	New York	NY	B
	Europe, India, US				
Travel Associates	800-992-7388	323-933-7388	Los Angeles	CA	B
	US, Hawaii, Caribbean				
Travel Avenue	800-333-3335	312-876-6866	Chicago	IL	P
	www.t100g.com				
	Worldwide, Canada, C. America (Mexico), Caribbean, US, rebate basis				
Travel Beyond	800-823-6063	612-475-2565	Wayzata	MN	B
	Africa (S. Africa)				
Travel Bound	800-456-8656	212-334-1350	New York	NY	B
	Europe, Asia				
Travel Center	800-419-0960	212-545-7474	New York	NY	B
	Asia, India				
Travel Center, Inc.	800-621-5228	312-726-0088	Chicago	IL	B
	Worldwide, Asia & Indian sub-continent, US				
Travel Charter	800-521-5267	248-641-9600	Troy	MI	B
	www.travelcharter.com				
	Charters to Europe, Caribbean, C. America (Mexico)				
Travel Desk	800-328-5377	612-835-9697	Bloomington	MN	B
	Worldwide, US, 1st & Business class				
Travel Express	800-333-3611	801-483-6120	Salt Lake City	UT	T
	Worldwide (exc. Canada & Mexico), US				

Travel Fore Seasons	800-328-1332	651-439-4634	Minnetonka	MN	P
	Europe (Eastern), CIS (Czech Air, Malev, Austrian, Moldova Airlines)				
Travel Impressions	800-284-0044	516-845-8000	Farmingdale	NY	T
	Europe, US (Florida, Las Vegas), Caribbean, C. & S. America, Hawaii				
Travel Leaders International (TLI)	800-323-3218	305-443-7755	Coral Gables	FL	T
	Worldwide (exc. Caribbean)				
Travel 'N Tours	800-984-9075	914-838-2600	Beacon	NY	B
	Worldwide (exc. Middle East, S. Pacific)				
Travel Network	800-338-7987	619-299-5161	San Diego	CA	B
	Asia				
Travel Network		423-485-1291	Chattanooga	TN	P
	www.airlineconsolidator.com				
	Worldwide				
Travel Network	800-929-1290	540-891-2929	Fredericksburg	VA	P
	www.travnet.com				
	Worldwide (exc. Middle East & Africa), US, hotels				
Travel Network	800-933-5963	425-643-1600	Bellevue	WA	P
	www.travel-network.com				
	US, Caribbean, C. & S. America				
Travel People	800-999-9912	305-596-4800	Miami	FL	B
	Europe, Russia, Africa, Asia, S. America, Caribbean				
Travel Planner	800-336-2757	216-831-9336	Beachwood	OH	B
	Europe, Middle East (Israel)				
Travel Team	800-788-0829	206-301-0443	Seattle	WA	P
	www.travelteam.com				
	Worldwide, US				
Travel Wholesalers International	800-487-8944	703-359-8855	Fairfax	VA	T
	www.owt.net				
	Europe, Russia, Middle East, Asia, C. & S. America, Caribbean (Aruba)				
Travel World	800-628-3002	407-628-2431	Winter Park	FL	B
	www.travelworlds.com				
	Africa, Middle East, India, Asia				
Traveline	800-992-9396		Cleveland	OH	B
	www.travelinetravel.com				
	S. Africa, Europe				
Travelink	800-525-2560	303-792-3124	Englewood	CO	T
	Worldwide				

Travnet Inc.	800-359-6388	312-836-9200	Chicago	IL	T
	www.travnet.net				
	Asia, S. Pacific				
Tread Lightly Ltd.	800-643-0060	860-868-1710	Wash. Depot	CT	B
	www.treadlightly.com				
	C. & S. America (exc. Mexico), Asia (Mongolia)				
Triple C Travel	800-638-9580	301-279-7652	Rockville	MD	B
	Asia, US				
Tulips Travel	800-882-3383	212-490-3388	New York	NY	B
	www.tulipstravel.com				
	S.E. Asia, Worldwide, US				
U.S.I. Travel	800-874-0073	773-404-0990	Chicago	IL	B
	800-759-7373	219-255-7272	Mishawaka	IN	
	Europe, Middle East				
Uniglobe Americana		504-561-8100	New Orleans	LA	B
	www.uniglobe.com				
	Worldwide, US				
Union Tours	800-451-9511	212-683-9500	New York	NY	T
	www.uniontours.com				
	Europe (Baltic States, Russia)				
Unique Travel	800-397-1719	503-221-1719	Portland	OR	B
	Asia, S. Pacific (via Korean Air), C. & S. America				
United Tours Corp.		212-245-1100	New York	NY	B
	Europe (Eastern, Russia via Aeroflot)				
Unitravel	800-325-2222	314-569-0900	St. Louis	MO	B
	www.unitravel.com				
	Worldwide, US (12% comission on available, published international fares)				
Unlimited World Travel	800-322-3557	708-442-7715	Lyons	IL	B
	Europe (Eastern), C. & S. America, Mexico				
Up and Away Travel	888-978-7629	323-852-9775	Beverly Hills	CA	T
		202-466-8900	Washington	DC	
		305-446-9997	Coral Gables	FL	
	l800-347-3813	617-236-8100	Boston	MA	
	l800-275-8001	212-889-2345	New York	NY	
	www.upandaway.com				
	Europe, Africa, Middle East, US				
Vacationland	800-245-0050	415-788-0503	San Francisco	CA	B
	www.vacation-land.com				
	S.E. Asia, Vietnam, Europe (London)				

Value Holidays	800-558-6850	414-241-6373	Mequon	WI	B
	www.valhol.com				
	Europe (Western), Worldwide				
Value Travel	800-887-5686	202-887-0065	Washington	DC	B
	C. & S. America				
Vytis Tours	800-778-9847	718-423-6161	Douglaston	NY	B
	www.vytistours.com				
	Europe (Scandinavia, Baltics, Russia)				
WalkerHill Worldwide Travel	800-568-2835	212-221-1234	New York	NY	B
	www.wwtny.com				
	Asia, Worldwide, US				
Way To Go Costa Rica	800-835-1223	919-782-1900	Raleigh	NC	T
	www.waytogocostarica.com				
	Costa Rica, C. & S. America, US, (American Airlines, Grupo Taca)				
Wholesale Travel	800-886-4988	703-379-1777	Falls Church	VA	T
	www.airfare.com				
	Europe, Middle East, Africa				
Winggate Travel		913-451-9200	Overland Park	KS	B
	www.winggatetravel.com				
	Asia				
World Connections	800-777-8892	770-393-8892	Atlanta	GA	B
	Asia, US				
World Trade Tours	800-732-7386	212-766-2288	New York	NY	B
	C. & S. America				
Worldvision Travel Services	800-545-7118	973-736-8210	West Orange	NJ	B
	www.worldvision.dntcj.ro				
	Europe, Africa, Asia, US				
Worldwide Travel, Inc.	800-343-0038	202-659-6430	Washington	DC	B
	800-820-8440	703-820-9700	Alexandria	VA	
	Worldwide, US				
Worldwide Travel - Pennsylvania	888-999-2394	717-394-6997	Lancaster	PA	B
	www.worldwidetravel.net				
	Europe				
WTT International	800-383-0556	212-532-0203	New York	NY	T
	S.E. Asia, Japan				
Zig Zag Travel	800-726-0249	718-575-3434	Rego Park	NY	B
	Worldwide, US				
Zohny Travel	800-963-6348	212-953-0077	New York	NY	B
	Middle East, Africa, Asia, India, US				

59

Chapter Three

Consolidators Who Sell to Travel Agents

The companies in this chapter are all marked "T" in the "Sells To" column in the main directory in Chapter 2. That means they sell exclusively to travel agents. All things being equal, consolidators that sell only to travel agents will offer the lowest net fares.

I have not included companies that indicated that they sell to both travel agents and the general public in this chapter (those marked "B" in the previous chapter). That is because those companies sometimes (but not always) sell to travel agents and the general public at exactly the same fare. That's not to say you can't find great net fares from those companies. If you are a travel agent interested in expanding your list of consolidators, it will be worth checking them out. However, when you are dealing with consolidators that sell exclusively to travel agents, you know you are getting the best fare they offer.

Arizona	Phoenix	Asian Travel
	Phoenix	Southwest Travel Systems
California	Beverly Hills	Up and Away Travel
	Glendale	African Travel
	Los Angeles	APC (Amer. Passenger Consol.)
	Los Angeles	C & H International

California (cont'd)	Los Angeles	Central Holidays Tours
	Los Angeles	Inta-Aussie Tours
	Los Angeles	Jetset Tours Inc.
	Los Angeles	PCS Travel
	Los Angeles	Picasso Travel
	Los Angeles	Skylink Travel
	Los Angeles	STT Worldwide Travel
	Los Angeles	Trans Am Travel
	Monterey	Pioneer Tours
	Receda	Hungarian Travel
	Sacramento	Diplomat Tours
	San Diego	J & O Air
	San Diego	Jetset Tours Inc.
	San Francisco	C & H International
	San Francisco	Jetset Tours Inc.
	San Francisco	Magical Holidays
	San Francisco	Picasso Travel
	San Francisco	Trans Am Travel
	San Jose	Apple Vacations
	San Jose	Charterways
	Santa Monica	Global Travel Consolidator
	Scotts Valley	Happy Tours Vacations
	Van Nuys	Brendan Air
Colorado	Englewood	Travelink
Dist of Columbia	Washington	C & H International
	Washington	Skylink Travel
	Washington	Solar Tours
	Washington	Up and Away Travel
Florida	Clermont	Jetset Tours Inc.
	Coral Gables	Getaway Travel
	Coral Gables	Prime Travel Services
	Coral Gables	Travel Leaders International (TLI)
	Coral Gables	Up and Away Travel
	Ft. Lauderdale	Cosmopolitan Travel Center
	Largo	Guardian Travel Service

Florida (cont'd)	Miami	Intervac
	Miami	Lomantours & Travel Service
	Miami	Mill-Run Tours
	Naples	Fare Game
	Sarasota	Solar Tours
Georgia	Atlanta	Everest Travel
	Atlanta	Golden Tour
	Atlanta	McAbee Tours
Illinois	Bensenville	Time Travel
	Chicago	C & H International
	Chicago	CES Travel
	Chicago	Compare Travel
	Chicago	Jetset Tours Inc.
	Chicago	Mill-Run Tours
	Chicago	Picasso Travel
	Chicago	Sky Bird Travel & Tours
	Chicago	Skylink Travel
	Chicago	Trans Am Travel
	Chicago	Travnet Inc.
	Elk Grove Village	Apple Vacations
Maryland	Baltimore	Europak Scan Division
Massachusetts	Boston	C & H International
	Boston	Picasso Travel
	Boston	Up and Away Travel
Michigan	East Lansing	AIT/Anderson International Travel
	Southfield	Sky Bird Travel & Tours
Minnesota	Minneapolis	Centrav, Inc.
	Minnetonka	MLT Vacations
	Minnetonka	Northwest WorldVacations
	Stillwater	Great Tours
Nebraska	Kearney	A Affordable Travel
Nevada	Las Vegas	Egypt National Tours & Travel
New Hampshire	Keene	General Tours
New Jersey	Englewood Cliffs	Mill-Run Tours
	Hasbrouck Hgts	International Travel Systems

N. Jersey (cont'd)	Rutherford	City Tours OBT
	West Orange	Agents Advantage
New York	Astoria	Plus Ultra Tours
	Astoria	Reko Tours
	Brooklyn	Ariel Tours, Inc.
	Farmingdale	Travel Impressions
	Hartsdale	American International Consol.
	Jericho	Caribbean Tours Specialists
	Jericho	Fantasy Holidays
	New York	Air Tickets
	New York	American Travel Abroad
	New York	APC (Amer. Passenger Consol.)
	New York	C & H International
	New York	CMM Travel
	New York	Council Wholesale
	New York	G A 2000
	New York	Hot Spot Tours
	New York	Inter-Island Tours
	New York	Ireland-UK Consolidated
	New York	Isram World of Travel
	New York	Italiatour
	New York	Jetset Tours Inc.
	New York	Mill-Run Tours
	New York	Picasso Travel
	New York	Sky Bird Travel & Tours
	New York	Skylink Travel
	New York	Sunrise Tours
	New York	Trans Am Travel
	New York	Union Tours
	New York	Up and Away Travel
	New York	WTT International
	Syosset	Sun Island Holidays
	Valley Stream	TAL Tours
North Carolina	Raleigh	Way To Go Costa Rica
Oregon	Beaverton	STT Worldwide Travel

Oregon (cont'd)	Portland	Avanti Destinations
	Portland	Pacific Gateway, Inc.
Pennsylvania	Glenside	Gate 1
	Philadelphia	Apple Vacations
	Philadelphia	HTI Tours
	Pittsburgh	Airplan
Texas	Dallas	GTT International
	Dallas	Middle East Travel Center
	Houston	C & H International
	Houston	Intratours
	Houston	Jetset Tours Inc.
	Houston	Middle East Travel Center
	Houston	Mill-Run Tours
Utah	Salt Lake City	Travel Express
Virginia	Alexandria	Best Travel
	Alexandria	Trans Am Travel
	Fairfax	Travel Wholesalers International
	Falls Church	Wholesale Travel
Washington	Seattle	Airmakers
	Seattle	Ausbound
	Seattle	C & H International
	Seattle	Jetset Tours Inc.
	Seattle	Marco Polo
	Seattle	Pacific Gateway, Inc.
CANADA		
British Columbia	Vancouver	Delights Travel
	Vancouver	Jade Tours
Ontario	Richmond Hill	Hillcrest Tours
	Toronto	CTI Carriers
	Toronto	G. G. Tours
	Toronto	Go Away Travel
Quebec	Montreal	Intair Transit

Chapter Four

Consolidators by Location

It's always a good idea to deal with a consolidator near you. There are a number of reasons for this, as I mentioned earlier: you can look over the consolidator's operation yourself, pick up your tickets in person, and complain immediately if there is a problem. It's also worth noting that not all consolidators offer tickets from multiple cities. Many only deal with flights that leave their city or region. Nothing irks a consolidator in Seattle more than receiving calls on the 800-line from "tire-kickers" in Miami.

Consolidators work on very thin margins. Respect them and the service they provide by not calling across the country unless absolutely necessary.

In this list, U.S. Consolidators are listed first, followed by their Canadian counterparts. Complete details on the companies listed will be found in the main directory in Chapter Two.

Alabama	Huntsville	Blueskies Travel
Arizona	Phoenix	Asian Travel
	Phoenix	Panda Travel
	Phoenix	Southwest Travel Systems
	Scottsdale	STA Travel
	Tempe	Adventure Bound Tours
	Tempe	Council Travel
	Tempe	STA Travel
	Tucson	Council Travel
Arkansas	Little Rock	First Discount Travel

California	Alhambra	APF Inc.
	Anaheim	Central Travel Network
	Berkeley	Council Travel
	Berkeley	STA Travel
	Beverly Hills	Air Travel Discounts
	Beverly Hills	Dloomy World Travel
	Beverly Hills	Professional Travel Service
	Beverly Hills	Senator Travel
	Beverly Hills	Up and Away Travel
	Concord	Global Adventures Travel
	Daly City	Custom Travel
	Davis	Council Travel
	El Segundo	South Star Tours
	Fremont	King Tut Tours, Inc.
	Fresno	Council Travel
	Fullerton	Council Travel
	Fullerton	K&K Travel
	Glendale	African Travel
	Hollywood	Supersonic Travel
	Irvine	Discover Wholesale Travel
	Isla Vista	Council Travel
	La Jolla	Council Travel
	Lakeport	Cheap Tickets
	Long Beach	Council Travel
	Los Angeles	All Continents Travel
	Los Angeles	APC
	Los Angeles	C & H International
	Los Angeles	Central Holidays Tours
	Los Angeles	Cheap Seats
	Los Angeles	Cheap Tickets
	Los Angeles	Council Travel
	Los Angeles	European Tours
	Los Angeles	Inta-Aussie Tours
	Los Angeles	Japan Express
	Los Angeles	Jetset Tours Inc.
	Los Angeles	Jetway Tours

California (cont'd)	Los Angeles	Levon Travel
	Los Angeles	New Frontiers West
	Los Angeles	PCS Travel
	Los Angeles	Picasso Travel
	Los Angeles	Sae Han Travel & Tours
	Los Angeles	Skylink Travel
	Los Angeles	STA Travel
	Los Angeles	STT Worldwide Travel
	Los Angeles	Tokyo Travel Service
	Los Angeles	Tradesco Tours
	Los Angeles	Trans Am Travel
	Monterey	Pioneer Tours
	Monterey Park	Cathay Travel
	N. Hollywood	Southern Connections
	Northridge	Council Travel
	Palo Alto	Council Travel
	Palo Alto	Scan The World
	Pasadena	Council Travel
	Pasadena	Holiday Tours
	Receda	Hungarian Travel
	Sacramento	Council Travel
	Sacramento	Diplomat Tours
	San Diego	1-800-FLYCHEAP
	San Diego	Central Travel Network
	San Diego	Council Travel
	San Diego	Fare Deal Travel
	San Diego	J & O Air
	San Diego	Jetset Tours Inc.
	San Diego	STA Travel
	San Diego	Travel Network
	San Francisco	Air Brokers International
	San Francisco	Airbound
	San Francisco	Alta Tours
	San Francisco	Aus Travel
	San Francisco	Avia Travel
	San Francisco	C & H International

California (cont'd)	San Francisco	Central Travel Network
	San Francisco	China Travel Service
	San Francisco	Council Travel
	San Francisco	Cut-Throat Travel
	San Francisco	Festival of Asia
	San Francisco	High Adventure
	San Francisco	Jetset Tours Inc.
	San Francisco	Magical Holidays
	San Francisco	Natrabu Indonesian Travel
	San Francisco	Palmair
	San Francisco	PCS Travel
	San Francisco	Picasso Travel
	San Francisco	Russart Travel
	San Francisco	Skytours Travel
	San Francisco	South Pacific Express Travel
	San Francisco	STA Travel
	San Francisco	Sun Destination Travel
	San Francisco	Ticket Planet
	San Francisco	Trans Am Travel
	San Francisco	Vacationland
	San Jose	Apple Vacations
	San Jose	Charterways
	San Jose	Suntrips
	Santa Ana	Aloha Continental Travel
	Santa Barbara	Council Travel
	Santa Clarita	Discount Travel
	Santa Monica	Continental Travel Shop
	Santa Monica	Flight Coordinators
	Santa Monica	Global Travel Consolidator
	Santa Monica	STA Travel
	Sausalito	The Budget Traveler
	Scotts Valley	Happy Tours Vacations
	Scotts Valley	Rockwell Tours
	Sherman Oaks	Brazil Tours
	Sun Valley	SITA World Travel
	Valencia	Rebel Tours & Travel

California (cont'd)	Van Nuys	Brendan Air
	Van Nuys	Central Travel Network
	Westminster	Lotus International Tours
Colorado	Aurora	Cheap Seats
	Aurora	Overseas Travel
	Aurora	Regatta Travel
	Boulder	Council Travel
	Denver	Affinity Travel
	Denver	Council Travel
	Denver	Mile High Tours
	Denver	Mr. Cheap's Travel
	Englewood	Fare Deals Travel
	Englewood	Travelink
Connecticut	New Haven	Council Travel
	New Milford	The Africa Desk
	Ridgefield	All Destinations
	Wash. Depot	Tread Lightly Ltd.
	Watertown	Accent on Africa
	Westport	Inclusive Holidays
	Wilton	International Ventures
Dist of Columbia	Washington	Americas Travel Services
	Washington	Bethany Travel Agency
	Washington	C & H International
	Washington	Council Travel
	Washington	Democracy Travel
	Washington	Fana Travels
	Washington	Ghana America Vacations
	Washington	PCS Travel
	Washington	PERS Travel Inc.
	Washington	Skylink Travel
	Washington	Solar Tours
	Washington	STA Travel
	Washington	Up and Away Travel
	Washington	Value Travel
	Washington	Worldwide Travel, Inc.
Florida	Boca Raton	Persvoyage

Florida (cont'd)	Boynton Beach	Palm Coast Travel
	Clermont	Jetset Tours Inc.
	Coral Gables	Getaway Travel
	Coral Gables	Interworld Travel
	Coral Gables	Karell Travel
	Coral Gables	Prime Travel Services
	Coral Gables	Queue Travel
	Coral Gables	STA Travel
	Coral Gables	Travel Leaders International (TLI)
	Coral Gables	Up and Away Travel
	Ft. Lauderdale	Aus Travel
	Ft. Lauderdale	Brazilian Wave Tours & Travel
	Ft. Lauderdale	Cosmopolitan Travel Center
	Ft. Lauderdale	Hostways Travel
	Ft. Lauderdale	North Star Tours
	Ft. Walton Beach	RTS Travel Services
	Gainesville	STA Travel
	Lake Worth	Intourist USA
	Largo	Guardian Travel Service
	Longwood	Latin Adventure Tours
	Miami	2000 Latin Tours
	Miami	4th Dimension Tours
	Miami	Council Travel
	Miami	Intervac
	Miami	Lomantours & Travel Service
	Miami	Mill-Run Tours
	Miami	Travel People
	Miami Beach	Mirabel Travel
	Naples	Europe On Line
	Naples	Fare Game
	Orlando	STA Travel
	Orlando	Travac Tours & Charters
	Sarasota	Solar Tours
	Tampa	Number One Travel
	Tampa	Passport Travel ManagementL
	Tampa	STA Travel

Florida (cont'd)	Vero Beach	Air Travel Discounts
	Winter Park	Travel World
Georgia	Atlanta	Council Travel
	Atlanta	Economy Travel
	Atlanta	Everest Travel
	Atlanta	Golden Tour
	Atlanta	Hari World Travel
	Atlanta	Japan Travel Service
	Atlanta	McAbee Tours
	Atlanta	Midtown Travel Consultants
	Atlanta	Regent Travel Network
	Atlanta	Skyway Travel
	Atlanta	South American Fiesta
	Atlanta	TMV Tours
	Atlanta	World Connections
	Marietta	Alpha Travel
	Norcross	China Professional Tours
Hawaii	Honolulu	Asia Travel Service
	Honolulu	Cheap Tickets
	Honolulu	Pali Tours & Travel
	Honolulu	Riverside Travel
Illinois	Bensenville	Time Travel
	Buffalo Grove	Hana Travel
	Carbondale	Borgsmiller Travels
	Carbondale	Malaysia Travel Advisors
	Chicago	C & H International
	Chicago	Central Travel Network
	Chicago	CES Travel
	Chicago	Chisholm Travel
	Chicago	Compare Travel
	Chicago	Council Travel
	Chicago	Egypt Tours & Travel
	Chicago	Hari World Travel
	Chicago	Jaya Travel
	Chicago	Jetset Tours Inc.
	Chicago	Mena Tours & Travel

Illinois (cont'd)	Chicago	Mill-Run Tours
	Chicago	National Travel Centre
	Chicago	Overseas Express
	Chicago	Picasso Travel
	Chicago	Sky Bird Travel & Tours
	Chicago	Skylink Travel
	Chicago	STA Travel
	Chicago	TMV Tours
	Chicago	Trade Wind Associates
	Chicago	Trans Am Travel
	Chicago	Travel Avenue
	Chicago	Travel Center, Inc.
	Chicago	Travnet Inc.
	Chicago	U.S.I. Travel
	Cicero	Central Travel Network
	Deerfield	Cut Rate Travel
	Elk Grove Village	Apple Vacations
	Evanston	Council Travel
	Lincolnshire	Safariline
	Lyons	Unlimited World Travel
	Rosemont	DER Travel Services
	Rosemont	Online Travel
Indiana	Bloomington	Council Travel
	Mishawaka	U.S.I. Travel
Iowa	Ames	Council Travel
	Cedar Rapids	Globe Travels
Kansas	Lawrence	Council Travel
	Overland Park	Dollar Saver Travel
	Overland Park	Winggate Travel
Louisiana	Baton Rouge	Discount Travel
	Baton Rouge	STA Travel
	New Orleans	Alp Reyal Tours
	New Orleans	Council Travel
	New Orleans	Uniglobe Americana
Maryland	Baltimore	AESU Travel
	Baltimore	Council Travel

Maryland (cont'd)	Baltimore	Europak Scan Division
	Bethesda	Dan Travel
	College Park	Council Travel
	Hanover	Student Travel Services
	Landover	Kambi Travel International
	Landover	Sharp Travel
	Owings Mills	Fare Deals Ltd.
	Rockville	Hans World Travel
	Rockville	Monica Travel & Tours
	Rockville	Triple C Travel
	Silver Spring	Sona Travels
Massachusetts	Amherst	Council Travel
	Boston	C & H International
	Boston	Council Travel
	Boston	Kutrubes Travel
	Boston	Picasso Travel
	Boston	Spector Travel
	Boston	STA Travel
	Boston	TMV Tours
	Boston	Up and Away Travel
	Cambridge	Council Travel
	Cambridge	STA Travel
Michigan	Ann Arbor	Council Travel
	Ann Arbor	STA Travel
	East Lansing	AIT/Anderson International Travel
	East Lansing	Council Travel
	Holland	GTI Travel Consolidators
	Southfield	Jaya Travel
	Southfield	Sky Bird Travel & Tours
	Troy	Travel Charter
Minnesota	Bloomington	Kristensen Int'l Travel & Tours
	Bloomington	Travel Desk
	Minneapolis	Campus Travel
	Minneapolis	Centrav, Inc.
	Minneapolis	Council Travel
	Minneapolis	STA Travel

Minn. (cont'd)	Minnetonka	MLT Vacations
	Minnetonka	Northwest World Vacations
	Minnetonka	Travel Fore Seasons
	Stillwater	Great Tours
	Wayzata	Travel Beyond
Missouri	Oak Grove	Group & Leisure Travel
	St. Louis	Unitravel
Montana	Kalispell	Integrity Travel
Nebraska	Kearney	A Affordable Travel
Nevada	Las Vegas	Central Travel Network
	Las Vegas	Egypt National Tours & Travel
	Las Vegas	Global Discount Travel Services
New Hampshire	Keene	General Tours
New Jersey	Bradley Bch	Alp Reyal Tours
	Cherry Hill	SAF Travel World
	Edison	Rupa Travel Service
	Edison	TMV Tours
	Englewood Cliffs	Central Holidays Tours
	Englewood Cliffs	Mill-Run Tours
	Fort Lee	Foreign Independent Tours
	Hackensack	Sunny Land Tours
	Hasbrouck Hgts	International Travel Systems
	Jersey City	Aviation Travels & Tours
	Jersey City	Garden State Travel
	Jersey City	Marakesh Tourist Company
	Jersey City	TMV Tours
	Millburn	Seamorgh Travel
	New Brunswick	Council Travel
	North Bergen	Gama Tours
	Parsippany	Paul Laifer Tours
	Rahway	Rahway Travel
	Ramsey	Prime Travel
	Rutherford	City Tours OBT
	West Orange	Agents Advantage
	West Orange	Gary Marcus Travel
	West Orange	Worldvision Travel Services

New York	Astoria	Crown Peters Travel
	Astoria	P&F International
	Astoria	Plus Ultra Tours
	Astoria	Reko Tours
	Beacon	Oxford Travel
	Beacon	Travel 'N Tours
	Brooklyn	Ariel Tours, Inc.
	Brooklyn	Falcon Travel & Tours
	Brooklyn	Favored Holidays
	Cedarhurst	Perfect Travel
	Douglaston	Vytis Tours
	Farmingdale	Travel Impressions
	Forest Hills	Spanish Heritage Tours
	Fresh Meadows	The Egyptian Connection
	Great Neck	F.O.S. Tours
	Hartsdale	American Int'l Consolidators
	Ithaca	Council Travel
	Jamaica	KTS Services
	Jericho	Caribbean Tours Specialists
	Jericho	Fantasy Holidays
	Lewiston	Raptim Travel
	New City	Pinto Basto USA
	New York	Air Tickets
	New York	Air Travel Discounts
	New York	Airfares
	New York	Air-Supply
	New York	Amba Travel
	New York	Am-Jet Travels
	New York	American Media Tours (AMT)
	New York	American Travel Abroad
	New York	ANA Hallo Tours
	New York	APC
	New York	Arkia Travel
	New York	Arrow Travel
	New York	ATC Travel
	New York	Aus Travel

New York (cont'd)	New York	Azure Travel Bureau
	New York	B & D Tours
	New York	Balkan USA
	New York	Brazilian Travel Service
	New York	C & H International
	New York	Calcos Tours
	New York	Carbone Travel
	New York	Central Europe Holidays
	New York	Cheap Tickets
	New York	Cloud Tours Travel
	New York	Club America Travel
	New York	CMM Travel
	New York	Council Travel
	New York	Council Wholesale
	New York	CWT Vacations
	New York	Dial Europe
	New York	Discount Tickets
	New York	Downtown Travel
	New York	Earth Travel
	New York	Ferns Travel
	New York	Fly Wise Travel
	New York	Flytime Tour & Travel
	New York	G A 2000
	New York	Glavs Travel
	New York	Global Journeys
	New York	Globe Travel Specialist
	New York	Hari World Travel
	New York	Himalayan International Tours
	New York	Homeric Tours & Charters
	New York	Hot Spot Tours
	New York	Inka's Empire Tours
	New York	Inter-Island Tours
	New York	International Travel Exchange
	New York	Ireland-UK Consolidated
	New York	Isram World of Travel
	New York	Italiatour

New York (cont'd)	New York	Jaya Travel
	New York	Jetset Tours Inc.
	New York	L. T. & Travel
	New York	Le Soleil Tours
	New York	Magical Holidays
	New York	Mercury Tours & Travel
	New York	Mill-Run Tours
	New York	Moment's Notice
	New York	Mr. Cheap's
	New York	Nefertai Travel
	New York	New Europe Holidays
	New York	New Frontiers USA
	New York	O'Connor Fairways Travel
	New York	Orbis Polish Travel
	New York	Pacific Holidays
	New York	Panorama Travel
	New York	Payless Travel
	New York	Peru Unlimited
	New York	Pharos Travel & Tourism
	New York	Picasso Travel
	New York	Pino Welcome Travel
	New York	Prestige Tour & Travel
	New York	Raj Travels
	New York	Sharp Travel Headquarters
	New York	Sky Bird Travel & Tours
	New York	Skylink Travel
	New York	STA Travel
	New York	Sunrise Tours
	New York	Super Travel & Tours
	New York	TFI Tours International
	New York	The French Experience
	New York	Tourlite International
	New York	Trade Wind Associates
	New York	Trans Am Travel
	New York	Travac Tours & Charters
	New York	Travel Abroad

New York (cont'd)	New York	Travel Bound
	New York	Travel Center
	New York	Tulips Travel
	New York	Union Tours
	New York	United Tours Corp.
	New York	Up and Away Travel
	New York	WalkerHill Worldwide Travel
	New York	World Trade Tours
	New York	WTT International
	New York	Zohny Travel
	Oceanside	Detours
	Rego Park	Zig Zag Travel
	Rockville Centre	Sceptre Tours & Charters
	Syosset	Sun Island Holidays
	Valley Stream	TAL Tours
	White Plains	Abratours
	White Plains	EuroGroups
	Yonkers	Benyo World Travel
North Carolina	Chapel Hill	Council Travel
	Raleigh	Way To Go Costa Rica
Ohio	Beachwood	Discover Africa
	Beachwood	Travel Planner
	Cleveland	American Travel
	Cleveland	Traveline
	Columbus	Council Travel
	Lakewood	Adventure Int'l Travel Service
	Lakewood	Panorama World Tours & Travel
	Woodmere	Elite Tours & Travel
Oregon	Aloha	First Discount Travel
	Beaverton	STT Worldwide Travel
	Clackamas	Mr. Cheap's Travel
	Eugene	Council Travel
	Portland	Avanti Destinations
	Portland	Council Travel
	Portland	Nova Travel
	Portland	Pacific Gateway, Inc.

Oregon (cont'd)	Portland	Unique Travel
Pennsylvania	Ardmore	DownUnder Direct
	Ardmore	Swain Australia Tours
	Glenside	Gate 1
	Lancaster	Worldwide Travel - Pennsylvania
	N. Huntingdon	Holiday Travel International
	Paoli	Pennsylvania Travel
	Philadelphia	Apple Vacations
	Philadelphia	Council Travel
	Philadelphia	HTI Tours
	Philadelphia	Premier Travel Services Inc.
	Philadelphia	SAF Travel World
	Philadelphia	STA Travel
	Pittsburgh	Airplan
	Pittsburgh	Council Travel
	Plymouth Meeting	1-800-Airfare
	State College	Council Travel
Rhode Island	Providence	Council Travel
Tennessee	Chattanooga	Travel Network
	Knoxville	Council Travel
Texas	Austin	Council Travel
	Austin	STA Travel
	College Station	ITS Tours & Travel
	Dallas	Air Discounters International
	Dallas	Central Travel Network
	Dallas	Council Travel
	Dallas	D-FW Tours
	Dallas	GTT International
	Dallas	Middle East Travel Center
	Dallas	Royal Lane Travel
	Dallas	TCI Travel
	Houston	Airfare Busters
	Houston	C & H International
	Houston	Council Travel
	Houston	EST International Travel
	Houston	Frosch International Travel

Texas (cont'd)	Houston	Intratours
	Houston	Jetset Tours Inc.
	Houston	Katy Van Tours
	Houston	Latin American Travel
	Houston	Middle East Travel Center
	Houston	Mill-Run Tours
	Houston	Tours International
	Houston	Trade Wind Associates
	Irving	Overseas Express
	Plano	Embassy Tours
	Trophy Club	Carefree Getaway Travel
Utah	Provo	Council Travel
	Salt Lake City	Council Travel
	Salt Lake City	Jensen Baron
	Salt Lake City	Travel Express
Virginia	Alexandria	Best Travel
	Alexandria	International Discount Travel
	Alexandria	Trans Am Travel
	Alexandria	Worldwide Travel, Inc.
	Annandale	Asia Specialists
	Annandale	Sharp Travel Agency
	Arlington	Gerosa Tours
	Arlington	Sona Travels
	Burke	Transview Travel
	Charlottesville	STA Travel
	Fairfax	Travel Wholesalers International
	Falls Church	Wholesale Travel
	Fredericksburg	Travel Network
	Richmond	Fellowship Travel International
Washington	Bellevue	Travel Network
	Seattle	Airmakers
	Seattle	Americas Tours
	Seattle	Around the World Travel
	Seattle	Ausbound
	Seattle	C & H International
	Seattle	Council Travel

Wash. (cont'd)	Seattle	Eastern Europe Tours
	Seattle	EZ Travel
	Seattle	Jetset Tours Inc.
	Seattle	Marco Polo
	Seattle	New Wave Travel
	Seattle	Pacific Gateway, Inc.
	Seattle	PCS Travel
	Seattle	Red Star Travel
	Seattle	STA Travel
	Seattle	Travel Team
Wisconsin	Madison	Council Travel
	Madison	STA Travel
	Mequon	Value Holidays
	Milwaukee	Pleasure Break Vacations
CANADA		
Alberta	Edmonton	Butte Travel Service
British Columbia	Richmond	Cannetic Travel
	Vancouver	Delights Travel
	Vancouver	Four Seasons Travel
	Vancouver	Jade Tours
	Vancouver	Pacesetter Travel
	Vancouver	Trade Wind Associates
	Victoria	Blaney's Travel Plus
Ontario	Kingston	Odyssey Travel
	North York	The Last Minute Club
	Ottawa	Odyssey Travel
	Richmond Hill	Hillcrest Tours
	Toronto	CTI Carriers
	Toronto	G. G. Tours
	Toronto	Go Away Travel
	Toronto	Trade Wind Associates
Quebec	Montreal	Chad & Calden
	Montreal	Intair Transit

Chapter Five

Consolidators by Destination

Use this listing to get a quick reading on which consolidators go where. Then turn to Chapter Two, *Consolidators in the U.S. and Canada,* for more detailed information, including web site addresses and a complete list of destinations each company offers.

Be aware that not every consolidator listed serves every country in the region. Those consolidators that offer tickets to a wide variety of worldwide destinations and do not specialize in any particular geographical area are listed under "Worldwide" (page 110).

Africa

A Affordable Travel	800-658-4366	308-234-2824	Kearney	NE T
Accent on Africa	888-237-4230	860-355-5800	Watertown	CT B
African Travel	800-421-8907	818-507-7893	Glendale	CA T
Air Tvl Discounts	800-888-2621	310-289-9761	Beverly Hills	CA B
		561-794-9345	Vero Beach	FL
		212-922-1326	New York	NY
Airplan	800-866-7526	412-257-3199	Pittsburgh	PA T
Air-Supply		212-695-1647	New York	NY P

AIT/Anderson	800-365-1929	517-337-1300	East Lansing	MI T
All Continents Tvl	800-368-6822	310-337-1641	Los Angeles	CA P
Alpha Travel	800-793-8424	770-988-9982	Marietta	GA B
Around the World	800-766-3601	206-223-3600	Seattle	WA B
Blueskies Travel	800-538-7597	256-551-1775	Huntsville	AL B
CES Travel	800-222-3020	312-922-2994	Chicago	IL T
Discover Africa	888-330-4880	216-595-9775	Beachwood	OH B
Dloomy World Tvl	800-356-6697	310-358-1400	Beverly Hills	CA B
Fana Travels	800-600-3262	202-667-0101	Washington	DC B
Foreign Indep.Trs	800-248-3487	201-585-1549	Fort Lee	NJ B
Frosch Int'l Travel	800-866-1623	713-850-1556	Houston	TX B
G A 2000	888-422-2216	212-903-3538	New York	NY T
Gate 1	800-682-3333	215-572-7676	Glenside	PA T
Ghana America	888-774-4262	202-862-4959	Washington	DC B
Go Away Travel	800-387-8850	416-322-1034	Toronto	ON T
Homeric Tours	800-223-5570	212-753-1100	New York	NY B
Int'l Travel Exchg	800-727-7830	212-808-5368	New York	NY B
Int'l Ventures	800-727-5475	203-761-1110	Wilton	CT B
Interworld Travel	800-468-3796	305-443-4929	Coral Gables	FL B
Kambi Travel Int'l	800-220-2192	301-925-9012	Landover	MD B
Karell Travel	800-327-0373	305-446-7766	Coral Gables	FL B
Le Soleil Tours	800-225-4723	212-687-2600	New York	NY B
Magical Holidays	800-433-7773	415-781-1345	San Francisco	CA T
Magical Holidays	800-235-4225	704-357-1820	Charlotte	NC B
	800-228-2208	212-486-9600	New York	NY
Middle East Tvl Ctr	800-672-0514	214-637-0514	Dallas	TX T
Monica Travel		301-294-1166	Rockville	MD B
Mr. Cheap's		212-431-1616	New York	NY P
Overseas Express	800-343-4873	773-262-4971	Chicago	IL B
	800-750-1224	972-819-2000	Irving	TX
Overseas Travel	800-783-7196	303-337-7196	Aurora	CO B
Oxford Travel	800-851-5290	914-838-1122	Beacon	NY B
Pacesetter Travel	800-663-5115	604-687-3083	Vancouver	BC P
Palmair	800-526-5892	415-826-8990	San Francisco	CA B
Payless Travel	800-892-0027	212-573-8986	New York	NY B
Pino Welcome	800-247-6578	212-682-5400	New York	NY B

Pleasure Break	800-777-1566	414-934-1882	Milwaukee	WI	B
Plus Ultra Tours	800-242-0394	718-278-1818	Astoria	NY	T
Premier Tvl Svcs	800-545-1910	215-893-9966	Philadelphia	PA	B
Prestige Tour	800-232-9638	212-779-8371	New York	NY	B
Safariline	877-723-2745	847-914-9300	Lincolnshire	IL	B
Scan The World		650-325-0876	Palo Alto	CA	B
SITA World Tvl		818-767-0039	Sun Valley	CA	P
Skylink Travel	800-247-6659	213-653-6718	Los Angeles	CA	T
Skyway Travel		404-252-2152	Atlanta	GA	B
Spector Travel	800-879-2374	617-338-0111	Boston	MA	B
TCI Travel	800-333-7033	214-630-3344	Dallas	TX	B
The Africa Desk	800-284-8796	860-354-9341	New Milford	CT	B
The Egypt. Conn.	800-334-4477	718-380-4330	Fresh Mdws	NY	B
TMV Tours		404-256-4809	Atlanta	GA	B
Travac Tours	800-872-8800	212-563-3303	New York	NY	B
Travel Beyond	800-823-6063	612-475-2565	Wayzata	MN	B
Travel Network	800-929-1290	540-891-2929	Fredericksburg	VA	P
Travel People	800-999-9912	305-596-4800	Miami	FL	B
Travel World	800-628-3002	407-628-2431	Winter Park	FL	B
Traveline	800-992-9396		Cleveland	OH	B
Up and Away	888-978-7629	323-852-9775	Beverly Hills	CA	T
		202-466-8900	Washington	DC	
		305-446-9997	Coral Gables	FL	
	800-347-3813	617-236-8100	Boston	MA	
	800-275-8001	212-889-2345	New York	NY	
Wholesale Travel	800-886-4988	703-379-1777	Falls Church	VA	T
Worldvision Travel	800-545-7118	973-736-8210	West Orange	NJ	B
Zohny Travel	800-963-6348	212-953-0077	New York	NY	B

Asia

1-800-Airfare	800-247-3273	610-834-8150	Plymouth Mtg	PA	B
Air Brokers Int'l	800-883-3273	415-397-1383	San Francisco	CA	B
Air Tvl Discounts	800-888-2621	310-289-9761	Beverly Hills	CA	B
		561-794-9345	Vero Beach	FL	
		212-922-1326	New York	NY	

Airplan	800-866-7526	412-257-3199	Pittsburgh	PA T
Air-Supply		212-695-1647	New York	NY P
Amba Travel		212-868-2500	New York	NY P
Am-Jet Travels	800-414-4147	212-697-5332	New York	NY B
ANA Hallo Tours	800-421-4136	212-399-6286	New York	NY B
APF Inc.	800-888-9168	626-282-9988	Alhambra	CA B
Around the World	800-766-3601	206-223-3600	Seattle	WA B
Asia Specialists	800-969-7427	703-941-2323	Annandale	VA B
Asia Travel Service		808-944-8811	Honolulu	HI B
Asian Travel	800-334-2742	602-954-0101	Phoenix	AZ T
Avanti Destinations	800-422-4256	503-295-1998	Portland	OR T
Avia Travel	800-950-2842	415-536-4155	San Francisco	CA P
Azure Tvl	800-882-1427	212-252-1056	New York	NY B
Best Travel	800-709-4545	703-924-9590	Alexandria	VA T
Blueskies Travel	800-538-7597	256-551-1775	Huntsville	AL B
Borgsmiller Travels	800-228-0585	618-529-5511	Carbondale	IL B
Cannetic Travel	888-279-9902	604-279-0066	Richmond	BC B
Carefree Getaway	800-969-8687	817-430-5828	Trophy Club	TX B
Cathay Travel		626-571-6727	Monterey Park	CA B
China Prof Tours	800-252-4462	770-849-0300	Norcross	GA B
China Travel Serv	800-899-8618	415-352-8618	San Francisco	CA P
Chisholm Travel	800-631-2824	312-321-1800	Chicago	IL P
CMM Travel	800-458-6663	212-557-1530	New York	NY T
Delights Travel		604-876-8278	Vancouver	BC T
Discover Whls Tvl	800-576-7770	949-833-1136	Irvine	CA P
Downtown Travel	800-952-3519	212-766-5705	New York	NY B
Earth Travel	800-203-1518	212-594-3553	New York	NY B
Festival of Asia	800-533-9953	415-908-6980	San Francisco	CA B
Flytime Tour	800-786-4388	212-760-3737	New York	NY B
Four Seasons Tvl		604-263-9915	Vancouver	BC P
Garden State Tvl		201-333-1232	Jersey City	NJ B
Gate 1	800-682-3333	215-572-7676	Glenside	PA T
Getaway Travel	800-683-6336	305-446-7855	Coral Gables	FL T
Glavs Travel	800-336-5727	212-290-3300	New York	NY B
Globe Travel	800-969-4562	212-843-9885	New York	NY B

Name	Phone 1	Phone 2	City	State	Type
Globe Travels		319-362-9071	Cedar Rapids	IA	P
Go Away Travel	800-387-8850	416-322-1034	Toronto	ON	T
Golden Tour	877-455-6888	770-455-8686	Atlanta	GA	T
GTI Travel Con.	800-829-8234	616-396-1234	Holland	MI	B
Hana Travel	800-962-8044	847-913-1177	Buffalo Grove	IL	B
Hans World Travel	800-421-4267	301-770-1717	Rockville	MD	B
Himalayan Int'l		212-564-5164	New York	NY	B
Int'l Travel Sys	800-258-0135	201-727-0470	Hasbr'ck Hgts	NJ	T
Intourist USA	800-556-5305	561-585-5305	Lake Worth	FL	B
ITS Tours & Travel	800-533-8688	409-764-0518	College Station	TX	B
Jade Tours	800-561-5233	604-689-5885	Vancouver	BC	T
Japan Express		213-680-0550	Los Angeles	CA	B
Japan Travel Service	800-822-3336	770-451-3607	Atlanta	GA	B
Jetway Tours	800-421-8771	818-990-2918	Los Angeles	CA	B
K&K Travel	800-523-1374	714-448-9678	Fullerton	CA	P
Kambi Tvl Int'l	800-220-2192	301-925-9012	Landover	MD	B
Katy Van Tours	800-808-8747	281-492-7032	Houston	TX	B
Malaysia Tvl Adv	800-359-8655	618-351-9398	Carbondale	IL	B
Marco Polo	800-831-3108	206-621-0700	Seattle	WA	T
Middle East Tvl Ctr	800-672-0514	214-637-0514	Dallas	TX	T
National Tvl Ctr	800-228-6886	312-939-2190	Chicago	IL	P
Natrabu Indonesian	800-628-7228	415-362-4225	San Francisco	CA	B
New Europe Hol	800-642-3874	212-686-2424	New York	NY	B
New Wave Travel	800-220-9283	206-527-3579	Seattle	WA	B
NW World Vacs	800-800-1504		Minnetonka	MN	P
	800-727-1111	612-470-1111	Minnetonka	MN	T
Nova Travel	800-334-1188	503-697-4460	Portland	OR	B
Number One Tvl	800-475-1009	813-872-6900	Tampa	FL	B
Overseas Express	800-343-4873	773-262-4971	Chicago	IL	B
	800-750-1224	972-819-2000	Irving	TX	B
Overseas Travel	800-783-7196	303-337-7196	Aurora	CO	B
Oxford Travel	800-851-5290	914-838-1122	Beacon	NY	B
Pacesetter Travel	800-663-5115	604-687-3083	Vancouver	BC	P
Pacific Holidays	800-355-8025	212-764-1977	New York	NY	B
Palm Coast Travel	800-444-1560	561-733-9950	Boynton Bch.	FL	B

Panorama Travel	800-204-7130	212-741-0033	New York	NY	B
Panorama World Tours & Travel	800-475-9339	216-228-9339	Lakewood	OH	B
Passport Travel	800-950-5864	813-931-3166	Tampa	FL	B
PCS Travel		213-239-2424	Los Angeles	CA	T
PCS Travel		213-239-2440	Los Angeles	CA	B
		415-972-8101	San Francisco	CA	
		202-833-3531	Washington	DC	
		206-682-8350	Seattle	WA	
Pino Welcome Tvl	800-247-6578	212-682-5400	New York	NY	B
Prime Travel	800-344-3962	201-825-1600	Ramsey	NJ	B
Raj Travels	888-359-4685	212-697-4612	New York	NY	B
Red Star Travel	800-215-4378		Seattle	WA	P
Regent Tvl Netwk		404-248-8062	Atlanta	GA	B
Sae Han Travel	800-421-5489	213-383-4988	Los Angeles	CA	B
SAF Travel World	800-394-8587	609-216-2900	Cherry Hill	NJ	B
Seamorgh Travel	800-543-2994	973-376-1141	Millburn	NJ	B
Sharp Travel	800-220-2165	301-731-3355	Landover	MD	B
Sharp Travel Agency	800-969-7427	703-941-2929	Annandale	VA	B
Sharp Travel Hq	800-252-1170	212-465-9500	New York	NY	B
SITA World Travel		818-767-0039	Sun Valley	CA	P
Skylink Travel	800-247-6659	213-653-6718	Los Angeles	CA	T
Skytours Travel	800-246-8687	415-228-8228	San Francisco	CA	B
Skyway Travel		404-252-2152	Atlanta	GA	B
S. Pacific Express	800-321-7739	415-982-6833	San Francisco	CA	B
Southwest Tvl Sys	800-314-6111	602-952-6900	Phoenix	AZ	T
STT Worldwide	800-975-1995	213-655-8866	Los Angeles	CA	T
	800-655-8866	503-641-8866	Beaverton	OR	
Sunrise Tours	800-872-3801	212-947-3617	New York	NY	T
Time Travel	800-847-7026	630-595-8463	Bensenville	IL	T
TMV Tours		404-256-4809	Atlanta	GA	B
Tokyo Travel Svc	800-227-2065	213-680-3545	Los Angeles	CA	B
Travac Tours	800-872-8800	212-563-3303	New York	NY	B
		407-896-0014	Orlando	FL	
Travel Bound	800-456-8656	212-334-1350	New York	NY	B
Travel Center	800-419-0960	212-545-7474	New York	NY	B

Travel Center, Inc.	800-621-5228	312-726-0088	Chicago	IL	B
Travel Network	800-338-7987	619-299-5161	San Diego	CA	B
Travel People	800-999-9912	305-596-4800	Miami	FL	B
Travel Whls Int'l	800-487-8944	703-359-8855	Fairfax	VA	T
Travel World	800-628-3002	407-628-2431	Winter Park	FL	B
Travnet Inc.	800-359-6388	312-836-9200	Chicago	IL	T
Tread Lightly Ltd.	800-643-0060	860-868-1710	Wash. Depot	CT	B
Triple C Travel	800-638-9580	301-279-7652	Rockville	MD	B
Tulips Travel	800-882-3383	212-490-3388	New York	NY	B
Unique Travel	800-397-1719	503-221-1719	Portland	OR	B
Vacationland	800-245-0050	415-788-0503	San Francisco	CA	B
WalkerHill W'wide	800-568-2835	212-221-1234	New York	NY	B
Winggate Travel		913-451-9200	Overland Park	KS	B
World Connections	800-777-8892	770-393-8892	Atlanta	GA	B
Worldvision Tvl Svc	800-545-7118	973-736-8210	West Orange	NJ	B
WTT International	800-383-0556	212-532-0203	New York	NY	T
Zohny Travel	800-963-6348	212-953-0077	New York	NY	B

Australia & South Pacific

Air Brokers In'tl	800-883-3273	415-397-1383	San Francisco	CA	B
Airmakers	800-841-4321	206-216-2914	Seattle	WA	T
Air-Supply		212-695-1647	New York	NY	P
Aus Travel	800-633-3404	415-781-4329	San Francisco	CA	P
	800-633-3404	954-525-6440	Ft. Lauderdale	FL	
	800-633-3404	212-972-6880	New York	NY	
Ausbound	800-345-5877		Seattle	WA	T
Blueskies Travel	800-538-7597	256-551-1775	Huntsville	AL	B
Chisholm Travel	800-631-2824	312-321-1800	Chicago	IL	P
Democracy Travel	800-536-8728	202-965-7200	Washington	DC	B
Discover Whls Tvl	800-576-7770	949-833-1136	Irvine	CA	P
DownUnder Direct	800-642-6224	610-896-1741	Ardmore	PA	B
Festival of Asia	800-533-9953	415-908-6980	San Francisco	CA	B
Global Adventures	800-989-6017	925-689-8883	Concord	CA	P
Global Travel Con.	800-366-3544	310-581-5610	Santa Monica	CA	T

Go Away Travel	800-387-8850	416-322-1034	Toronto	ON	T
Happy Tours Vacs	800-877-4277	408-461-0013	Scotts Valley	CA	T
Inta-Aussie Tours	800-531-9222	310-568-2060	Los Angeles	CA	T
Int'l Discount Tvl	800-466-7357	703-750-0101	Alexandria	VA	B
Int'l Travel Sys	800-258-0135	201-727-0470	Hasbr'k Hgts	NJ	T
K&K Travel	800-523-1374	714-448-9678	Fullerton	CA	P
Kristensen Int'l	800-262-8728	612-854-5589	Bloomington	MN	P
National Travel Ctr	800-228-6886	312-939-2190	Chicago	IL	P
Odyssey Travel		613-549-3553	Kingston	ON	P
		613-789-1900	Ottawa	ON	
Pacesetter Travel	800-663-5115	604-687-3083	Vancouver	BC	P
Panorama World	800-475-9339	216-228-9339	Lakewood	OH	B
Passport Travel	800-950-5864	813-931-3166	Tampa	FL	B
Payless Travel	800-892-0027	212-573-8986	New York	NY	B
Scan The World		650-325-0876	Palo Alto	CA	B
S. Pacific Express	800-321-7739	415-982-6833	San Francisco	CA	B
Southwest Tvl Sys	800-314-6111	602-952-6900	Phoenix	AZ	T
Swain Australia	800-227-9246	610-896-9595	Ardmore	PA	B
Ticket Planet	800-799-8888	415-288-9999	San Francisco	CA	B
Travac Tours	800-872-8800	407-896-0014	Orlando	FL	B
Travel 'N Tours	800-984-9075	914-838-2600	Beacon	NY	B
Travnet Inc.	800-359-6388	312-836-9200	Chicago	IL	T
Unique Travel	800-397-1719	503-221-1719	Portland	OR	B

Central & South America

1-800-Airfare	800-247-3273	610-834-8150	Plymouth Mtg	PA	B
2000 Latin Tours	800-254-7378	305-670-4488	Miami	FL	B
4th Dimension	800-343-0020	305-279-0014	Miami	FL	B
Agents Advantage	800-816-2211	908-355-2222	West Orange	NJ	T
Air Tickets	800-207-7300	212-557-3275	New York	NY	T
Airplan	800-866-7526	412-257-3199	Pittsburgh	PA	T
All Continents Tvl	800-368-6822	310-337-1641	Los Angeles	CA	P
All Destinations	800-228-1510	203-744-3100	Ridgefield	CT	B
Alta Tours	800-338-4191	415-777-1307	San Francisco	CA	B

Americas Tours	800-553-2513	206-623-8850	Seattle	WA P
Americas Tvl Svcs	800-704-6484	202-955-3815	Washington	DC B
Apple Vacations	800-800-0202	408-452-0202	San Jose	CA T
	800-365-2776	847-640-1150	Elk Grove Vill	IL
	800-727-3400	610-359-6700	Philadelphia	PA
Around the World	800-766-3601	206-223-3600	Seattle	WA B
ATC Travel	800-826-6388	212-967-1200	New York	NY B
Avanti Destinations	800-422-4256	503-295-1998	Portland	OR T
Bethany Travel		202-223-3336	Washington	DC B
Blaney's Tvl Plus	800-376-6177	250-382-7254	Victoria	BC P
Brazil Tours	800-927-8352	818-990-4995	Sherman Oaks	CA B
Brazilian Tvl Svc	800-342-5746	212-764-6161	New York	NY B
Brazilian Wave	800-682-3315	954-561-3788	Ft. Lauderdale	FL B
Calcos Tours		212-889-9200	New York	NY B
Carbone Travel	800-735-8899	212-213-4310	New York	NY B
Central Tvl Netwk		714-520-4535	Anaheim	CA B
		619-239-9090	San Diego	CA
		415-285-0288	San Francisco	CA
		818-785-8844	Van Nuys	CA
		312-368-8288	Chicago	IL
		708-656-1190	Cicero	IL
		702-388-1663	Las Vegas	NV
		214-943-5400	Dallas	TX
Cheap Seats	800-451-7200	818-717-8591	Los Angeles	CA P
City Tours OBT	800-238-2489	201-939-6572	Rutherford	NJ T
Compare Travel	800-532-9939	312-853-1144	Chicago	IL T
Cosmopolitan Tvl	800-548-7206	954-523-0973	Ft. Lauderdale	FL T
Dan Travel	800-362-1308	301-907-8977	Bethesda	MD B
Eastern Europe Trs	800-441-1339	206-448-8400	Seattle	WA B
Embassy Tours	800-299-5284	972-985-2929	Plano	TX B
Ferns Travel	800-790-1016	212-868-9194	New York	NY B
General Tours	800-221-2216		Keene	NH T
Gerosa Tours	800-243-7672	703-415-4795	Arlington	VA B
Getaway Travel	800-683-6336	305-446-7855	Coral Gables	FL T
Globe Travel Spec	800-969-4562	212-843-9885	New York	NY B
Happy Tours Vacs	800-877-4277	408-461-0013	Scotts Valley	CA T
Holiday Tours	800-393-1212	626-795-1012	Pasadena	CA B

Company	Phone 1	Phone 2	City	State	Type
Inka's Empire Tours		212-875-0370	New York	NY	B
Int'l Discount Tvl	800-466-7357	703-750-0101	Alexandria	VA	B
Interworld Travel	800-468-3796	305-443-4929	Coral Gables	FL	B
Intratours	800-334-8069	713-952-0662	Houston	TX	T
Jetway Tours	800-421-8771	818-990-2918	Los Angeles	CA	B
Katy Van Tours	800-808-8747	281-492-7032	Houston	TX	B
Latin Adventure Trs	888-293-0780	407-339-9296	Longwood	FL	B
Latin American Tvl	800-252-0775	713-774-0600	Houston	TX	B
Lomantours & Tvl	800-344-8054	305-573-4011	Miami	FL	T
Mena Tours & Tvl	800-937-6362	773-275-2125	Chicago	IL	B
Mile High Tours	800-777-8687	303-758-8246	Denver	CO	B
MLT Vacations	800-328-0025	612-672-3111	Minnetonka	MN	T
Monica Travel		301-294-1166	Rockville	MD	B
Mr. Cheap's		212-431-1616	New York	NY	P
NW World Vacs	800-800-1504		Minnetonka	MN	P
Online Travel	800-660-5300	847-318-8890	Rosemont	IL	P
Overseas Travel	800-783-7196	303-337-7196	Aurora	CO	B
Oxford Travel	800-851-5290	914-838-1122	Beacon	NY	B
P&F International	800-444-6666	718-937-1998	Astoria	NY	B
Palm Coast Travel	800-444-1560	561-733-9950	Boynton Bch.	FL	B
Peru Unlimited	800-947-5655	212-995-9786	New York	NY	B
Pino Welcome Tvl	800-247-6578	212-682-5400	New York	NY	B
Pinto Basto USA	800-526-8539	914-639-8020	New City	NY	B
Pioneer Tours	800-288-2107	408-648-8800	Monterey	CA	T
Pleasure Break	800-777-1566	414-934-1882	Milwaukee	WI	B
Prime Travel Svcs	800-447-4013	305-441-0622	Coral Gables	FL	T
Professional Travel	800-289-0549	323-852-0549	Beverly Hills	CA	B
Queue Travel	800-356-4871	305-445-7740	Coral Gables	FL	B
Rockwell Tours	800-526-4910	831-461-0133	Scotts Valley	CA	B
Skytours Travel	800-246-8687	415-228-8228	San Francisco	CA	B
Solar Tours	800-388-7652	202-861-5864	Washington	DC	T
	800-727-7652	941-966-1664	Sarasota	FL	T
Sona Travels	800-720-7662	301-589-3344	Silver Spring	MD	B
	800-721-7662	703-528-6644	Arlington	VA	B
S. American Fiesta	800-334-3782	770-321-6814	Atlanta	GA	B
South Star Tours	800-654-4468	310-416-1001	El Segundo	CA	B

Southern Connects	800-635-3303	818-508-8899	N. Hollywood	CA	P
Southwest Tvl Sys	800-314-6111	602-952-6900	Phoenix	AZ	T
Suntrips	800-786-8747	408-432-1101	San Jose	CA	B
TFI Tours Int'l	800-745-8000	212-736-1140	New York	NY	B
The Budget Travlr		415-331-3700	Sausalito	CA	B
Tokyo Travel Svc	800-227-2065	213-680-3545	Los Angeles	CA	B
Tourlite Int'l	800-272-7600	212-599-2727	New York	NY	B
Tours International	800-247-7965	713-223-5544	Houston	TX	B
Travac Tours	800-872-8800	212-563-3303	New York	NY	B
Travel Avenue	800-333-3335	312-876-6866	Chicago	IL	P
Travel Charter	800-521-5267	248-641-9600	Troy	MI	B
Travel Impressions	800-284-0044	516-845-8000	Farmingdale	NY	T
Travel Network	800-933-5963	425-643-1600	Bellevue	WA	P
Travel People	800-999-9912	305-596-4800	Miami	FL	B
Travel Whls Int'l	800-487-8944	703-359-8855	Fairfax	VA	T
Tread Lightly Ltd.	800-643-0060	860-868-1710	Wash. Depot	CT	B
Unique Travel	800-397-1719	503-221-1719	Portland	OR	B
Unlimited World Tvl	800-322-3557	708-442-7715	Lyons	IL	B
Value Travel	800-887-5686	202-887-0065	Washington	DC	B
Way To Go C.R.	800-835-1223	919-782-1900	Raleigh	NC	T
World Trade Tours	800-732-7386	212-766-2288	New York	NY	B

Caribbean

All Destinations	800-228-1510	203-744-3100	Ridgefield	CT	B
Am. Media Tours	800-969-6344	212-465-1630	New York	NY	B
Apple Vacations	800-800-0202	408-452-0202	San Jose	CA	T
	800-365-2776	847-640-1150	Elk Grove Vill	IL	
	800-727-3400	610-359-6700	Philadelphia	PA	
Butte Travel Svc	800-661-8906	780-477-3561	Edmonton	AB	P
Caribbean Tours	800-930-9021	516-827-9884	Jericho	NY	T
Centrav, Inc.	800-874-2033	612-948-8400	Minneapolis	MN	T
D-FW Tours	800-527-2589	972-980-4540	Dallas	TX	B
Fare Deals Ltd.	800-347-7006	410-581-8787	Owings Mills	MD	P
G. G. Tours	800-504-5557	416-487-1146	Toronto	ON	T

Gary Marcus Tvl	800-524-0821	973-731-7600	West Orange	NJ	B
Hillcrest Tours	800-268-3820	905-884-1832	Richmond Hill	ON	T
Hot Spot Tours	800-433-0075	212-421-9090	New York	NY	T
Inclusive Holidays	800-238-2140	203-454-2233	Westport	CT	B
Inter-Island Tours	800-245-3434	212-686-4868	New York	NY	T
Intervac	800-992-9629	305-670-8990	Miami	FL	T
L. T. & Travel	800-295-3436	212-682-2748	New York	NY	B
Latin Adventure Trs	888-293-0780	407-339-9296	Longwood	FL	B
Latin American Tvl	800-252-0775	713-774-0600	Houston	TX	B
Mena Tours & Tvl	800-937-6362	773-275-2125	Chicago	IL	B
MLT Vacations	800-328-0025	612-672-3111	Minnetonka	MN	T
NW World Vacs	800-800-1504		Minnetonka	MN	P
Rockwell Tours	800-526-4910	831-461-0133	Scotts Valley	CA	B
Student Tvl Svcs	800-648-4849	410-859-4200	Hanover	MD	B
Sun Isl. Holidays	800-824-4653	516-364-4000	Syosset	NY	T
Travel Associates	800-992-7388	323-933-7388	Los Angeles	CA	B
Travel Avenue	800-333-3335	312-876-6866	Chicago	IL	P
Travel Charter	800-521-5267	248-641-9600	Troy	MI	B
Travel Impressions	800-284-0044	516-845-8000	Farmingdale	NY	T
Travel Leaders Int'l	800-323-3218	305-443-7755	Coral Gables	FL	T
Travel Network	800-933-5963	425-643-1600	Bellevue	WA	P
Travel People	800-999-9912	305-596-4800	Miami	FL	B
Travel Whls Int'l	800-487-8944	703-359-8855	Fairfax	VA	T

Europe

1-800-Airfare	800-247-3273	610-834-8150	Plymouth Mtg	PA	B
4th Dimension	800-343-0020	305-279-0014	Miami	FL	B
Abratours	800-227-2887	914-949-3300	White Plains	NY	B
Adventure Int'l	800-542-2487	216-228-7171	Lakewood	OH	B
AESU Travel	800-638-7640	410-366-5494	Baltimore	MD	B
Agents Advantage	800-816-2211	908-355-2222	West Orange	NJ	T
Air Tvl Discounts	800-888-2621	310-289-9761	Beverly Hills	CA	B
	800-888-2621	561-794-9345	Vero Beach	FL	
	800-888-2621	212-922-1326	New York	NY	

Airfares	800-753-0578	212-213-3865	New York	NY	B
Airplan	800-866-7526	412-257-3199	Pittsburgh	PA	T
Air-Supply		212-695-1647	New York	NY	P
AIT/Anderson	800-365-1929	517-337-1300	East Lansing	MI	T
All Continents Tvl	800-368-6822	310-337-1641	Los Angeles	CA	P
Aloha Continental	800-287-0275	714-565-3737	Santa Ana	CA	B
Alp Reyal Tours	800-853-3058	504-488-4146	New Orleans	LA	B
	877-988-8802	732-988-8814	Bradley Bch	NJ	
Alpha Travel	800-793-8424	770-988-9982	Marietta	GA	B
Alta Tours	800-338-4191	415-777-1307	San Francisco	CA	B
Amba Travel		212-868-2500	New York	NY	P
Am Int'l Consol	800-888-5774	914-682-5679	Hartsdale	NY	T
Am Media Tours	800-969-6344	212-465-1630	New York	NY	B
American Travel		216-781-7181	Cleveland	OH	B
Amer Tvl Abroad	800-228-0877	212-586-5230	New York	NY	T
Around the World	800-766-3601	206-223-3600	Seattle	WA	B
ATC Travel	800-826-6388	212-967-1200	New York	NY	B
Avanti Destinations	800-422-4256	503-295-1998	Portland	OR	T
Balkan USA	800-822-1106	212-338-6838	New York	NY	B
Benyo World Tvl	800-872-8925	914-968-0175	Yonkers	NY	B
Blaney's Tvl Pluss	800-376-6177	250-382-7254	Victoria	BC	P
Blueskies Travel	800-538-7597	256-551-1775	Huntsville	AL	B
Butte Travel Svc	800-661-8906	780-477-3561	Edmonton	AB	P
Campus Travel	800-328-3359	612-338-5616	Minneapolis	MN	B
Carefree Getaway	800-969-8687	817-430-5828	Trophy Club	TX	B
Central Europe Hol	800-800-8891	212-725-0948	New York	NY	B
Central Holidays	800-935-5000	310-216-5777	Los Angeles	CA	T
	800-935-5000	201-228-5200	Englew'd Cliffs	NJ	B
Cheap Seats	800-451-7200	818-717-8591	Los Angeles	CA	P
Cloud Tours Travel	800-223-7880	212-753-6104	New York	NY	B
Cont'l Travel Shop		310-453-8655	Santa Monica	CA	B
Cosmopolitan Tvl	800-548-7206	954-523-0973	Ft. Lauderdale	FL	T
Crown Peters Tvl	800-321-1199	718-932-7800	Astoria	NY	B
CTI Carriers	800-363-8181	416-429-9000	Toronto	ON	T
Discount Travel		310-641-5343	Santa Clarita	CA	P
Discover Whls Tvl	800-576-7770	949-833-1136	Irvine	CA	P

Dloomy World Tvl	800-356-6697	310-358-1400	Beverly Hills	CA	B
Downtown Travel	800-952-3519	212-766-5705	New York	NY	B
Eastern Eur Tours	800-441-1339	206-448-8400	Seattle	WA	B
EuroGroups	800-462-2577	914-682-7456	White Plains	NY	B
Europak Scan Div	800-253-1342		Baltimore	MD	T
Europe On Line	800-587-4849	941-263-3937	Naples	FL	B
European Tours	800-882-3983	213-624-9378	Los Angeles	CA	B
F.O.S. Tours	800-367-3450	516-466-5651	Great Neck	NY	B
Fana Travels	800-600-3262	202-667-0101	Washington	DC	B
Fantasy Holidays	800-645-2555	516-935-8500	Jericho	NY	T
Fare Deal Travel	800-243-2785	619-282-8866	San Diego	CA	P
Favored Holidays		718-934-8881	Brooklyn	NY	B
Ferns Travel	800-790-1016	212-868-9194	New York	NY	B
Flytime Tour & Tvl	800-786-4388	212-760-3737	New York	NY	B
G A 2000	888-422-2216	212-903-3538	New York	NY	T
Gama Tours	800-747-7235	201-662-1000	N. Bergen	NJ	B
Gate 1	800-682-3333	215-572-7676	Glenside	PA	T
General Tours	800-221-2216		Keene	NH	T
Gerosa Tours	800-243-7672	703-415-4795	Arlington	VA	B
Getaway Travel	800-683-6336	305-446-7855	Coral Gables	FL	T
Glavs Travel	800-336-5727	212-290-3300	New York	NY	B
Globe Travel	800-969-4562	212-843-9885	New York	NY	B
Globe Travels		319-362-9071	Cedar Rapids	IA	P
Great Tours	800-607-7066	651-439-0690	Stillwater	MN	T
GTI Travel Con	800-829-8234	616-396-1234	Holland	MI	B
Guardian Tvl Svc	800-741-3050	727-585-3322	Largo	FL	T
Hans World Travel	800-421-4267	301-770-1717	Rockville	MD	B
Hari World Travel		404-233-5005	Atlanta	GA	B
		773-381-5555	Chicago	IL	
		212-957-3000	New York	NY	
Hillcrest Tours	800-268-3820	905-884-1832	Richmond Hill	ON	T
Homeric Tours	800-223-5570	212-753-1100	New York	NY	B
Hungarian Travel	800-624-9277	818-996-3510	Receda	CA	T
Inclusive Holidays	800-238-2140	203-454-2233	Westport	CT	B
Int'l Discount Tvl	800-466-7357	703-750-0101	Alexandria	VA	B
Int'l Travel Exchg	800-727-7830	212-808-5368	New York	NY	B

Int'l Travel Sys	800-258-0135	201-727-0470	Hasbr'ck Hgts	NJ	T
Interworld Travel	800-468-3796	305-443-4929	Coral Gables	FL	B
Intourist USA	800-556-5305	561-585-5305	Lake Worth	FL	B
Intratours	800-334-8069	713-952-0662	Houston	TX	T
Ireland-UK Consol	888-577-2900	212-661-1999	New York	NY	T
Italiatour	800-237-0517	212-903-3300	New York	NY	T
ITS Tours & Travel	800-533-8688	409-764-0518	College Station	TX	B
Jetway Tours	800-421-8771	818-990-2918	Los Angeles	CA	B
K&K Travel	800-523-1374	714-448-9678	Fullerton	CA	P
Kambi Travel Int'l	800-220-2192	301-925-9012	Landover	MD	B
Katy Van Tours	800-808-8747	281-492-7032	Houston	TX	B
KTS Services	800-531-6677	718-454-2300	Jamaica	NY	B
Kutrubes Travel	800-878-8566	617-426-5668	Boston	MA	B
Le Soleil Tours	800-225-4723	212-687-2600	New York	NY	B
Levon Travel	800-445-3866	323-871-8711	Los Angeles	CA	B
Magical Holidays	800-235-4225	704-357-1820	Charlotte	NC	B
	800-228-2208	212-486-9600	New York	NY	
Marakesh Tourist	800-458-1772	201-435-2800	Jersey City	NJ	B
Middle East Tvl Ctr	800-672-0514	214-637-0514	Dallas	TX	T
Mirabel Travel	800-890-4590	305-937-4880	Miami Beach	FL	B
Monica Travel		301-294-1166	Rockville	MD	B
Mr. Cheap's Travel	800-672-4327	303-758-3833	Denver	CO	P
	800-672-4327	503-557-9101	Clackamas	OR	
Nefertai Travel	888-616-3337	212-697-5563	New York	NY	B
New Europe Hol	800-642-3874	212-686-2424	New York	NY	B
New Frontiers USA	800-366-6387	212-779-0600	New York	NY	B
New Frontiers West	800-677-0720	310-670-7318	Los Angeles	CA	B
North Star Tours	800-431-1511	954-776-7070	Ft. Lauderdale	FL	B
NW World Vacs	800-800-1504		Minnetonka	MN	P
O'Connor Fairways	800-662-0550	212-661-0550	New York	NY	P
Online Travel	800-660-5300	847-318-8890	Rosemont	IL	P
Orbis Polish Travel	800-867-6526	212-867-5011	New York	NY	B
Overseas Express	800-343-4873	773-262-4971	Chicago	IL	B
	800-750-1224	972-819-2000	Irving	TX	
Overseas Travel	800-783-7196	303-337-7196	Aurora	CO	B
Oxford Travel	800-851-5290	914-838-1122	Beacon	NY	B

P&F International	800-444-6666	718-937-1998	Astoria	NY	B
Palm Coast Travel	800-444-1560	561-733-9950	Boynton Bch.	FL	B
Palmair	800-526-5892	415-826-8990	San Francisco	CA	B
Panorama Travel	800-204-7130	212-741-0033	New York	NY	B
Panorama World	800-475-9339	216-228-9339	Lakewood	OH	B
Paul Laifer Tours	800-346-6314	973-887-1188	Parsippany	NJ	B
Payless Travel	800-892-0027	212-573-8986	New York	NY	B
Persvoyage	888-455-7377	561-347-0900	Boca Raton	FL	B
Pharos Travel	877-999-5511	212-736-6070	New York	NY	B
Pino Welcome Tvl	800-247-6578	212-682-5400	New York	NY	B
Pinto Basto USA	800-526-8539	914-639-8020	New City	NY	B
Pleasure Break	800-777-1566	414-934-1882	Milwaukee	WI	B
Plus Ultra Tours	800-242-0394	718-278-1818	Astoria	NY	T
Prime Travel	800-344-3962	201-825-1600	Ramsey	NJ	B
Queue Travel	800-356-4871	305-445-7740	Coral Gables	FL	B
Rahway Travel	800-526-2786	732-381-8800	Rahway	NJ	B
Raj Travels	888-359-4685	212-697-4612	New York	NY	B
Rebel Tours & Tvl	800-227-3235	661-294-0900	Valencia	CA	B
Red Star Travel	800-215-4378		Seattle	WA	P
Russart Travel	888-338-7877	415-781-6655	San Francisco	CA	P
SAF Travel World	800-394-8587	609-216-2900	Cherry Hill	NJ	B
Scan The World		650-325-0876	Palo Alto	CA	B
Senator Travel	800-736-2121	323-782-9500	Beverly Hills	CA	B
Skylink Travel	800-247-6659	213-653-6718	Los Angeles	CA	T
Skytours Travel	800-246-8687	415-228-8228	San Francisco	CA	B
Skyway Travel		404-252-2152	Atlanta	GA	B
Solar Tours	800-388-7652	202-861-5864	Washington	DC	T
	800-727-7652	941-966-1664	Sarasota	FL	
Sona Travels	800-720-7662	301-589-3344	Silver Spring	MD	B
	800-721-7662	703-528-6644	Arlington	VA	
S. Pacific Express	800-321-7739	415-982-6833	San Francisco	CA	B
Southwest Tvll Sys	800-314-6111	602-952-6900	Phoenix	AZ	T
Spanish Heritage	800-221-2580	718-544-2752	Forest Hills	NY	B
STT Worldwide Tvl	800-975-1995	213-655-8866	Los Angeles	CA	T
	800-655-8866	503-641-8866	Beaverton	OR	
Sunrise Tours	800-872-3801	212-947-3617	New York	NY	T

Suntrips	800-786-8747	408-432-1101	San Jose	CA	B
TCI Travel	800-333-7033	214-630-3344	Dallas	TX	B
TFI Tours Int'l	800-745-8000	212-736-1140	New York	NY	B
The Budget Travlr		415-331-3700	Sausalito	CA	B
The Egyptian Conn	800-334-4477	718-380-4330	Fresh Mdws	NY	B
The French Exp		212-986-3800	New York	NY	P
Time Travel	800-847-7026	630-595-8463	Bensenville	IL	T
Tokyo Travel Svc	800-227-2065	213-680-3545	Los Angeles	CA	B
Tradesco Tours	800-833-3402	310-649-5808	Los Angeles	CA	B
Travac Tours	800-872-8800	212-563-3303	New York	NY	B
Travel Abroad	800-297-8788	212-564-8989	New York	NY	B
Travel Bound	800-456-8656	212-334-1350	New York	NY	B
Travel Charter	800-521-5267	248-641-9600	Troy	MI	B
Tvl Fore Seasons	800-328-1332	651-439-4634	Minnetonka	MN	P
Travel Impressions	800-284-0044	516-845-8000	Farmingdale	NY	T
Travel People	800-999-9912	305-596-4800	Miami	FL	B
Travel Planner	800-336-2757	216-831-9336	Beachwood	OH	B
Travel Whls Int'l	800-487-8944	703-359-8855	Fairfax	VA	T
Traveline	800-992-9396		Cleveland	OH	B
U.S.I. Travel	800-874-0073	773-404-0990	Chicago	IL	B
	800-759-7373	219-255-7272	Mishawaka	IN	
Union Tours	800-451-9511	212-683-9500	New York	NY	T
United Tours Corp.		212-245-1100	New York	NY	B
Unlimited World Tvl	800-322-3557	708-442-7715	Lyons	IL	B
Up and Away	888-978-7629	323-852-9775	Beverly Hills	CA	T
		202-466-8900	Washington	DC	
		305-446-9997	Coral Gables	FL	
	800-347-3813	617-236-8100	Boston	MA	
	800-275-8001	212-889-2345	New York	NY	
Vacationland	800-245-0050	415-788-0503	San Francisco	CA	B
Value Holidays	800-558-6850	414-241-6373	Mequon	WI	B
Vytis Tours	800-778-9847	718-423-6161	Douglaston	NY	B
Wholesale Travel	800-886-4988	703-379-1777	Falls Church	VA	T
Worldvision Travel	800-545-7118	973-736-8210	West Orange	NJ	B
Worldwide Tvl - PA	888-999-2394	717-394-6997	Lancaster	PA	B

Hawaii

Apple Vacations	800-800-0202	408-452-0202	San Jose	CA	T
	800-365-2776	847-640-1150	Elk Grove Vill	IL	
	800-727-3400	610-359-6700	Philadelphia	PA	
Butte Travel Svc	800-661-8906	780-477-3561	Edmonton	AB	P
Central Tvl Netwk		714-520-4535	Anaheim	CA	B
		619-239-9090	San Diego	CA	
		415-285-0288	San Francisco	CA	
		818-785-8844	Van Nuys	CA	
		312-368-8288	Chicago	IL	
		708-656-1190	Cicero	IL	
		702-388-1663	Las Vegas	NV	
		214-943-5400	Dallas	TX	
D-FW Tours	800-527-2589	972-980-4540	Dallas	TX	B
Fantasy Holidays	800-645-2555	516-935-8500	Jericho	NY	T
Fare Deals Ltd.	800-347-7006	410-581-8787	Owings Mills	MD	P
Happy Tours Vacs	800-877-4277	408-461-0013	Scotts Valley	CA	T
Jetset Tours Inc.	800-638-3273	323-290-5800	Los Angeles	CA	T
L. T. & Travel	800-295-3436	212-682-2748	New York	NY	B
Moment's Notice		212-486-0500	New York	NY	P
Suntrips	800-786-8747	408-432-1101	San Jose	CA	B
Travel Associates	800-992-7388	323-933-7388	Los Angeles	CA	B
Travel Impressions	800-284-0044	516-845-8000	Farmingdale	NY	T

India, Nepal, Pakistan

Am-Jet Travels	800-414-4147	212-697-5332	New York	NY	B
Amba Travel		212-868-2500	New York	NY	P
Around the World	800-766-3601	206-223-3600	Seattle	WA	B
Azure Tvl Bureau	800-882-1427	212-252-1056	New York	NY	B
Dollar Saver Tvl		913-381-5050	Overland Park	KS	P
Fana Travels	800-600-3262	202-667-0101	Washington	DC	B
Gate 1	800-682-3333	215-572-7676	Glenside	PA	T
General Tours	800-221-2216		Keene	NH	T
Globe Travels		319-362-9071	Cedar Rapids	IA	P

Hari World Travel		404-233-5005	Atlanta	GA	B
		773-381-5555	Chicago	IL	
		212-957-3000	New York	NY	
Himalayan Int'l		212-564-5164	New York	NY	B
ITS Tours & Travel	800-533-8688	409-764-0518	College Station	TX	B
NW World Vacs	800-800-1504		Minnetonka	MN	P
Nova Travel	800-334-1188	503-697-4460	Portland	OR	B
Raj Travels	888-359-4685	212-697-4612	New York	NY	B
Sharp Travel Agcy	800-969-7427	703-941-2929	Annandale	VA	B
SITA World Travel		818-767-0039	Sun Valley	CA	P
Sona Travels	800-720-7662	301-589-3344	Silver Spring	MD	B
	800-721-7662	703-528-6644	Arlington	VA	
Super Travel	800-878-7371	212-986-8002	New York	NY	B
TMV Tours		404-256-4809	Atlanta	GA	B
Transview Travel	800-553-6762	703-912-3900	Burke	VA	B
Travel Abroad	800-297-8788	212-564-8989	New York	NY	B
Travel Center	800-419-0960	212-545-7474	New York	NY	B
Travel Center, Inc.	800-621-5228	312-726-0088	Chicago	IL	B
Travel World	800-628-3002	407-628-2431	Winter Park	FL	B
Zohny Travel	800-963-6348	212-953-0077	New York	NY	B

Middle East & Mediterranean

Abratours	800-227-2887	914-949-3300	White Plains	NY	B
Affinity Travel	888-733-4726	303-639-1000	Denver	CO	B
Air Tvl Discounts	800-888-2621	310-289-9761	Beverly Hills	CA	B
	800-888-2621	561-794-9345	Vero Beach	FL	
	800-888-2621	212-922-1326	New York	NY	
Airplan	800-866-7526	412-257-3199	Pittsburgh	PA	T
All Continents Tvl	800-368-6822	310-337-1641	Los Angeles	CA	P
Alp Reyal Tours	800-853-3058	504-488-4146	New Orleans	LA	B
	877-988-8802	732-988-8814	Bradley Bch	NJ	
Alpha Travel	800-793-8424	770-988-9982	Marietta	GA	B
Am-Jet Travels	800-414-4147	212-697-5332	New York	NY	B
Ariel Tours, Inc.	800-262-1818	718-633-7900	Brooklyn	NY	T
B & D Tours	800-548-6877	212-953-3300	New York	NY	B

Central Holidays	800-935-5000	310-216-5777	Los Angeles	CA	T
Central Holidays	800-935-5000	201-228-5200	Englew'd Cliffs	NJ	B
Club America Tvl	800-221-4969	212-972-2865	New York	NY	B
Crown Peters Tvl	800-321-1199	718-932-7800	Astoria	NY	B
Dloomy World Tvl	800-356-6697	310-358-1400	Beverly Hills	CA	B
Egypt Tours & Tvl	800-523-4978	773-506-9999	Chicago	IL	B
Elite Tours & Tvl	800-354-8320	216-514-9000	Woodmere	OH	B
EZ Travel		206-524-1977	Seattle	WA	B
Fana Travels	800-600-3262	202-667-0101	Washington	DC	B
Foreign Indep Trs	800-248-3487	201-585-1549	Fort Lee	NJ	B
Frosch Int'l Travel	800-866-1623	713-850-1556	Houston	TX	B
G A 2000	888-422-2216	212-903-3538	New York	NY	T
Gama Tours	800-747-7235	201-662-1000	N. Bergen	NJ	B
Gate 1	800-682-3333	215-572-7676	Glenside	PA	T
General Tours	800-221-2216		Keene	NH	T
Global Journeys	888-743-6999	212-221-0710	New York	NY	B
Guardian Tvl Svc	800-741-3050	727-585-3322	Largo	FL	T
Homeric Tours	800-223-5570	212-753-1100	New York	NY	B
Int'l Travel Exchg	800-727-7830	212-808-5368	New York	NY	B
Int'l Travel Sys	800-258-0135	201-727-0470	Hasbr'k Hgts	NJ	T
Isram World of Tvl	800-223-7460	212-983-8381	New York	NY	T
Katy Van Tours	800-808-8747	281-492-7032	Houston	TX	B
Kutrubes Travel	800-878-8566	617-426-5668	Boston	MA	B
Levon Travel	800-445-3866	323-871-8711	Los Angeles	CA	B
Lotus Int'l Tours	800-450-4638	714-892-8502	Westminster	CA	B
Marakesh Tourist	800-458-1772	201-435-2800	Jersey City	NJ	B
Middle East Tvl Ctr	800-672-0514	214-637-0514	Dallas	TX	T
Mirabel Travel	800-890-4590	305-937-4880	Miami Beach	FL	B
Monica Travel		301-294-1166	Rockville	MD	B
Nefertai Travel	888-616-3337	212-697-5563	New York	NY	B
New Europe Hol	800-642-3874	212-686-2424	New York	NY	B
Online Travel	800-660-5300	847-318-8890	Rosemont	IL	P
Overseas Express	800-343-4873	773-262-4971	Chicago	IL	B
	800-750-1224	972-819-2000	Irving	TX	
Overseas Travel	800-783-7196	303-337-7196	Aurora	CO	B
P&F International	800-444-6666	718-937-1998	Astoria	NY	B

Palmair	800-526-5892	415-826-8990	San Francisco	CA	B
Panorama World	800-475-9339	216-228-9339	Lakewood	OH	B
Perfect Travel	800-352-5359	516-791-9089	Cedarhurst	NY	B
PERS Travel Inc.	800-583-0909	202-338-2121	Washington	DC	B
Persvoyage	888-455-7377	561-347-0900	Boca Raton	FL	B
Pharos Travel	877-999-5511	212-736-6070	New York	NY	B
Pleasure Break	800-777-1566	414-934-1882	Milwaukee	WI	B
Prime Travel	800-344-3962	201-825-1600	Ramsey	NJ	B
Safariline	877-723-2745	847-914-9300	Lincolnshire	IL	B
Skylink Travel	800-247-6659	213-653-6718	Los Angeles	CA	T
Skyway Travel		404-252-2152	Atlanta	GA	B
Sona Travels	800-720-7662	301-589-3344	Silver Spring	MD	B
	800-721-7662	703-528-6644	Arlington	VA	
Sunrise Tours	800-872-3801	212-947-3617	New York	NY	T
TAL Tours	800-825-9399	516-825-0966	Valley Stream	NY	T
TCI Travel	800-333-7033	214-630-3344	Dallas	TX	B
The Egyptian Conn	800-334-4477	718-380-4330	Fresh Mdws	NY	B
TMV Tours		404-256-4809	Atlanta	GA	B
Tourlite Int'l	800-272-7600	212-599-2727	New York	NY	B
Travac Tours	800-872-8800	212-563-3303	New York	NY	B
Travel 'N Tours	800-984-9075	914-838-2600	Beacon	NY	B
Travel Network	800-929-1290	540-891-2929	Fredericksburg	VA	P
Travel Planner	800-336-2757	216-831-9336	Beachwood	OH	B
Travel Whls Int'l	800-487-8944	703-359-8855	Fairfax	VA	T
Travel World	800-628-3002	407-628-2431	Winter Park	FL	B
U.S.I. Travel	800-874-0073	773-404-0990	Chicago	IL	B
	800-759-7373	219-255-7272	Mishawaka	IN	
Up and Away	888-978-7629	323-852-9775	Beverly Hills	CA	T
		202-466-8900	Washington	DC	
		305-446-9997	Coral Gables	FL	
	800-347-3813	617-236-8100	Boston	MA	
	800-275-8001	212-889-2345	New York	NY	
Wholesale Travel	800-886-4988	703-379-1777	Falls Church	VA	T
Zohny Travel	800-963-6348	212-953-0077	New York	NY	B

Round-the-World & Circle Pacific

Air Brokers Int'l	800-883-3273	415-397-1383	San Francisco	CA	B
Around the World	800-766-3601	206-223-3600	Seattle	WA	B
Avia Travel	800-950-2842	415-536-4155	San Francisco	CA	P
Council Travel		510-848-8604	Berkeley	CA	P
		562-621-6603	Long Beach	CA	
		310-208-3551	Los Angeles	CA	
		650-325-3888	Palo Alto	CA	
		619-270-6401	San Diego	CA	
		415-421-3473	San Francisco	CA	
		805-562-8080	Santa Barbara	CA	
		203-562-5335	New Haven	CT	
		202-337-6464	Washington	DC	
		305-670-9261	Miami	FL	
		404-377-9997	Atlanta	GA	
		812-330-1600	Bloomington	IN	
		413-256-1261	Amherst	MA	
		617-266-1926	Boston	MA	
		617-497-1497	Cambridge	MA	
		410-516-0560	Baltimore	MD	
		301-779-1172	College Park	MD	
		734-998-0200	Ann Arbor	MI	
		919-942-2334	Chapel Hill	NC	
		212-822-2700	New York	NY	
		503-228-1900	Portland	OR	
		215-382-0343	Philadelphia	PA	
		814-861-3232	State College	PA	
		401-331-5810	Providence	RI	
		423-974-9200	Knoxville	TN	
		206-632-2448	Seattle	WA	
		206-329-4567	Seattle	WA	
Democracy Travel	800-536-8728	202-965-7200	Washington	DC	B
Global Adventures	800-989-6017	925-689-8883	Concord	CA	P
High Adventure	800-350-0612	415-912-5600	San Francisco	CA	B
Odyssey Travel		613-549-3553	Kingston	ON	P
		613-789-1900	Ottawa	ON	
Scan The World		650-325-0876	Palo Alto	CA	B
Ticket Planet	800-799-8888	415-288-9999	San Francisco	CA	B

United States

1-800-Airfare	800-247-3273	610-834-8150	Plymouth Mtg	PA	B
1-800-FLYCHEAP	800-359-24327		San Diego	CA	P
Agents Advantage	800-816-2211	908-355-2222	West Orange	NJ	T
Air Discounters Int'l	800-527-2589	972-980-4540	Dallas	TX	P
All Destinations	800-228-1510	203-744-3100	Ridgefield	CT	B
Aloha Continental	800-287-0275	714-565-3737	Santa Ana	CA	B
Alpha Travel	800-793-8424	770-988-9982	Marietta	GA	B
Am-Jet Travels	800-414-4147	212-697-5332	New York	NY	B
Am Int'l Consol	800-888-5774	914-682-5679	Hartsdale	NY	T
Am Media Tours	800-969-6344	212-465-1630	New York	NY	B
APC	800-933-4421	323-655-6121	Los Angeles	CA	T
	888-971-0006	212-972-1558	New York	NY	
Arkia Travel		212-557-1587	New York	NY	B
Asia Travel Svc		808-944-8811	Honolulu	HI	B
Ausbound	800-345-5877		Seattle	WA	T
Blaney's Tvl Plus	800-376-6177	250-382-7254	Victoria	BC	P
Brazilian Tvl Svc	800-342-5746	212-764-6161	New York	NY	B
Carefree Getaway	800-969-8687	817-430-5828	Trophy Club	TX	B
Central Holidays	800-935-5000	310-216-5777	Los Angeles	CA	T
Central Holidays	800-935-5000	201-228-5200	Englew'd Cliffs	NJ	B
Cheap Seats	888-221-2727	303-338-5558	Aurora	CO	B
CWT Vacations	800-223-6862	212-695-8435	New York	NY	B
D-FW Tours	800-527-2589	972-980-4540	Dallas	TX	B
Discount Tickets	888-382-4327	212-391-2313	New York	NY	B
Discount Travel	888-738-8747	504-761-4711	Baton Rouge	LA	P
Economy Travel	888-222-2110	770-290-7730	Atlanta	GA	P
Egypt Nat'l Tours	877-993-4978	702-696-0084	Las Vegas	NV	T
EZ Travel		206-524-1977	Seattle	WA	B
Fana Travels	800-600-3262	202-667-0101	Washington	DC	B
Fare Deal Travel	800-243-2785	619-282-8866	San Diego	CA	P
Fare Deals Ltd.	800-347-7006	410-581-8787	Owings Mills	MD	P
Fare Deals Travel	800-878-2929	303-792-2929	Englewood	CO	P
Fly Wise Travel	800-347-3939	212-869-2223	New York	NY	B
Gary Marcus Tvl	800-524-0821	973-731-7600	West Orange	NJ	B

Global Discount	800-497-6678		Las Vegas	NV	P
Group & Leisure	800-874-6608	816-690-4040	Oak Grove	MO	P
GTT International	800-878-4283	972-960-2000	Dallas	TX	T
Hari World Travel		404-233-5005	Atlanta	GA	B
		773-381-5555	Chicago	IL	
		212-957-3000	New York	NY	
Hillcrest Tours	800-268-3820	905-884-1832	Richmond Hill	ON	T
Holiday Travel Int'l	800-775-7111	724-863-7500	N. Huntingdon	PA	B
Hungarian Travel	800-624-9277	818-996-3510	Receda	CA	T
Intair Transit		514-286-7078	Montreal	PQ	T
Int'l Travel Exchg	800-727-7830	212-808-5368	New York	NY	B
Jade Tours	800-561-5233	604-689-5885	Vancouver	BC	T
Jaya Travel	877-359-5292	312-606-9600	Chicago	IL	P
		248-372-4800	Southfield	MI	
		212-697-0022	New York	NY	
Jetset Tours Inc.	800-638-3273	323-290-5800	Los Angeles	CA	T
L. T. & Travel	800-295-3436	212-682-2748	New York	NY	B
Levon Travel	800-445-3866	323-871-8711	Los Angeles	CA	B
Mercury Tours	877-711-8687	212-268-7434	New York	NY	B
Mile High Tours	800-777-8687	303-758-8246	Denver	CO	B
MLT Vacations	800-328-0025	612-672-3111	Minnetonka	MN	T
Moment's Notice		212-486-0500	New York	NY	P
Mr. Cheap's		212-431-1616	New York	NY	P
Mr. Cheap's Travel	800-672-4327	303-758-3833	Denver	CO	P
Mr. Cheap's Travel	800-672-4327	503-557-9101	Clackamas	OR	P
Nefertai Travel	888-616-3337	212-697-5563	New York	NY	B
NW World Vacs	800-800-1504		Minnetonka	MN	P
Nova Travel	800-334-1188	503-697-4460	Portland	OR	B
Odyssey Travel		613-549-3553	Kingston	ON	P
		613-789-1900	Ottawa	ON	
Pacific Gateway	800-777-8369	503-294-6478	Portland	OR	T
	800-777-8369	206-624-2228	Seattle	WA	
Panda Travel	800-447-2632	602-943-3383	Phoenix	AZ	P
Payless Travel	800-892-0027	212-573-8986	New York	NY	B
Pennsylvania Tvl	800-331-0947	610-251-9944	Paoli	PA	P
Pharos Travel	877-999-5511	212-736-6070	New York	NY	B
Pino Welcome	800-247-6578	212-682-5400	New York	NY	B

Regatta Travel	800-445-7685	303-751-0666	Aurora	CO	P
Rupa Travel Svc		732-572-5000	Edison	NJ	B
SAF Travel World	800-394-8587	609-216-2900	Cherry Hill	NJ	B
Scan The World		650-325-0876	Palo Alto	CA	B
Sharp Travel	800-220-2165	301-731-3355	Landover	MD	B
Sharp Travel Agcy	800-969-7427	703-941-2929	Annandale	VA	B
Sky Bird Travel	887-759-2473	312-606-9600	Chicago	IL	T
	887-759-2473	248-372-4800	Southfield	MI	
	887-759-2473	212-697-0022	New York	NY	
Sona Travels	800-720-7662	301-589-3344	Silver Spring	MD	B
	800-721-7662	703-528-6644	Arlington	VA	
S. Pacific Express	800-321-7739	415-982-6833	San Francisco	CA	B
STT Worldwide Tvl	800-975-1995	213-655-8866	Los Angeles	CA	T
	800-655-8866	503-641-8866	Beaverton	OR	
Sun Destination Tvl		415-398-1313	San Francisco	CA	P
Supersonic Travel		323-851-0333	Hollywood	CA	B
TFI Tours Int'l	800-745-8000	212-736-1140	New York	NY	B
The Last Min Club	800-563-2582	416-441-2582	North York	ON	P
Trade Wind Assoc	800-268-4853	604-683-6900	Vancouver	BC	B
	800-438-4853	312-664-3434	Chicago	IL	
	800-438-4853	212-286-0667	New York	NY	
	800-268-4853	416-966-4853	Toronto	ON	
	800-438-4853	713-960-0343	Houston	TX	
Travel Abroad	800-297-8788	212-564-8989	New York	NY	B
Travel Associates	800-992-7388	323-933-7388	Los Angeles	CA	B
Travel Avenue	800-333-3335	312-876-6866	Chicago	IL	P
Travel Center, Inc.	800-621-5228	312-726-0088	Chicago	IL	B
Travel Desk	800-328-5377	612-835-9697	Bloomington	MN	B
Travel Express	800-333-3611	801-483-6120	Salt Lake City	UT	T
Travel Impressions	800-284-0044	516-845-8000	Farmingdale	NY	T
Travel Network	800-929-1290	540-891-2929	Fredericksburg	VA	P
Travel Network	800-933-5963	425-643-1600	Bellevue	WA	P
Travel Team	800-788-0829	206-301-0443	Seattle	WA	P
Triple C Travel	800-638-9580	301-279-7652	Rockville	MD	B
Tulips Travel	800-882-3383	212-490-3388	New York	NY	B
Uniglobe Amer		504-561-8100	New Orleans	LA	B
Unitravel	800-325-2222	314-569-0900	St. Louis	MO	B

Up and Away	888-978-7629	323-852-9775	Beverly Hills	CA	T
		202-466-8900	Washington	DC	
		305-446-9997	Coral Gables	FL	
	800-347-3813	617-236-8100	Boston	MA	
	800-275-8001	212-889-2345	New York	NY	
WalkerHill W'wide	800-568-2835	212-221-1234	New York	NY	B
Way To Go C.R.	800-835-1223	919-782-1900	Raleigh	NC	T
World Connections	800-777-8892	770-393-8892	Atlanta	GA	B
Worldvision Tvl Svc	800-545-7118	973-736-8210	West Orange	NJ	B
Worldwide Travel	800-343-0038	202-659-6430	Washington	DC	B
	800-820-8440	703-820-9700	Alexandria	VA	
Zig Zag Travel	800-726-0249	718-575-3434	Rego Park	NY	B
Zohny Travel	800-963-6348	212-953-0077	New York	NY	B

Worldwide

Adventure Bound		602-968-7889	Tempe	AZ	B
Air Discounters	800-527-2589	972-980-4540	Dallas	TX	P
Air Tickets	800-207-7300	212-557-3275	New York	NY	T
Airbound		415-834-9445	San Francisco	CA	P
Airfare Busters	800-232-8783	713-961-5109	Houston	TX	B
Airmakers	800-841-4321	206-216-2914	Seattle	WA	T
APC	800-933-4421	323-655-6121	Los Angeles	CA	T
	888-971-0006	212-972-1558	New York	NY	
Arkia Travel		212-557-1587	New York	NY	B
Arrow Travel		212-889-2550	New York	NY	P
Aviation Travels		201-418-8167	Jersey City	NJ	P
Bethany Tvl Agcy		202-223-3336	Washington	DC	B
Brazilian Tvl Svc	800-342-5746	212-764-6161	New York	NY	B
Brendan Air	800-491-9633	818-785-9696	Van Nuys	CA	T
C & H International	800-833-8888	323-933-2288	Los Angeles	CA	T
	800-289-1628	415-956-2288	San Francisco	CA	
		202-223-2288	Washington	DC	
		312-346-2828	Chicago	IL	
		617-357-1608	Boston	MA	
		212-219-9300	New York	NY	
	888-440-2288	713-272-0006	Houston	TX	
	888-808-2288		Seattle	WA	

Cathay Travel		626-571-6727	Monterey Park	CA	B
Centrav, Inc.	800-874-2033	612-948-8400	Minneapolis	MN	T
Chad & Calden		514-729-0111	Montreal	PQ	P
Charterways	800-869-2344	408-257-2652	San Jose	CA	T
Cheap Tickets	800-377-1000		Lakeport	CA	P
	800-377-1000	310-645-5054	Los Angeles	CA	
	800-377-1000	808-947-3717	Honolulu	HI	
	800-377-1000	212-570-1179	New York	NY	
Compare Travel	800-532-9939	312-853-1144	Chicago	IL	T
Council Travel	800-226-8624	(nat'l. res. ctr.)	Boston	MA	P
		602-966-3544	Tempe	AZ	
		520-881-8345	Tucson	AZ	
		510-848-8604	Berkeley	CA	
		530-752-2285	Davis	CA	
		209-278-6623	Fresno	CA	
		714-278-2157	Fullerton	CA	
		805-562-8080	Isla Vista	CA	
		619-452-0630	La Jolla	CA	
		562-621-6603	Long Beach	CA	
		310-208-3551	Los Angeles	CA	
		818-882-4692	Northridge	CA	
		650-325-3888	Palo Alto	CA	
		626-793-5595	Pasadena	CA	
		916-278-4224	Sacramento	CA	
		619-270-6401	San Diego	CA	
		415-421-3473	San Francisco	CA	
		805-562-8080	Santa Barbara	CA	
		303-447-8101	Boulder	CO	
		303-571-0630	Denver	CO	
		203-562-5335	New Haven	CT	
		202-337-6464	Washington	DC	
		305-670-9261	Miami	FL	
		404-377-9997	Atlanta	GA	
		515-296-2326	Ames	IA	
		312-951-0585	Chicago	IL	
		847-475-5070	Evanston	IL	
		812-330-1600	Bloomington	IN	
		785-749-3900	Lawrence	KS	
		504-866-1767	New Orleans	LA	
		413-256-1261	Amherst	MA	
		617-266-1926	Boston	MA	
		617-497-1497	Cambridge	MA	
		410-516-0560	Baltimore	MD	

Council Travel		301-779-1172	College Park	MD P
(cont'd)		734-998-0200	Ann Arbor	MI
		517-432-7722	East Lansing	MI
		612-379-2323	Minneapolis	MN
		919-942-2334	Chapel Hill	NC
		732-249-6667	New Brunswk	NJ
		607-277-0373	Ithaca	NY
		212-666-4177	New York	NY
		212-254-2525	New York	NY
		212-822-2700	New York	NY
		614-294-8697	Columbus	OH
		541-344-2263	Eugene	OR
		503-228-1900	Portland	OR
		215-382-0343	Philadelphia	PA
		412-683-1881	Pittsburgh	PA
		814-861-3232	State College	PA
		401-331-5810	Providence	RI
		423-974-9200	Knoxville	TN
		512-472-4931	Austin	TX
		214-363-9941	Dallas	TX
		713-743-2777	Houston	TX
		801-375-1919	Provo	UT
		801-582-5840	Salt Lake City	UT
		206-632-2448	Seattle	WA
		206-329-4567	Seattle	WA
		608-280-8906	Madison	WI
Council Wholesale	800-347-2433	212-822-2800	New York	NY T
Custom Travel	800-535-9797	415-239-4200	Daly City	CA B
Cut Rate Travel	800-388-0575	847-405-0575	Deerfield	IL B
Cut-Throat Travel		415-989-8747	San Francisco	CA P
CWT Vacations	800-223-6862	212-695-8435	New York	NY B
D-FW Tours	800-527-2589	972-980-4540	Dallas	TX B
Democracy Travel	800-536-8728	202-965-7200	Washington	DC B
DER Travel Svcs	800-717-4247	847-430-0000	Rosemont	IL B
Detours	800-252-8780	516-763-1900	Oceanside	NY B
Dial Europe		212-758-5310	New York	NY B
Diplomat Tours	800-727-8687	916-972-1500	Sacramento	CA T
Discount Travel	888-738-8747	504-761-4711	Baton Rouge	LA P
Dollar Saver Tvl		913-381-5050	Overland Park	KS P
Economy Travel	888-222-2110	770-290-7730	Atlanta	GA P
Egypt Nat'l Tours	877-993-4978	702-696-0084	Las Vegas	NV T

EST Int'l Travel		713-974-0521	Houston	TX B
Everest Travel		770-220-1866	Atlanta	GA T
EZ Travel		206-524-1977	Seattle	WA B
Falcon Travel	800-272-6394	718-522-0692	Brooklyn	NY B
Fare Deals Ltd.	800-347-7006	410-581-8787	Owings Mills	MD P
Fare Deals Travel	800-878-2929	303-792-2929	Englewood	CO P
Fare Game		941-430-1440	Naples	FL T
Fellowship Tvl Int'l	800-446-7667	804-264-0121	Richmond	VA B
First Discount Tvl	800-951-9558	501-219-1893	Little Rock	AR P
	888-819-4646	503-848-4646	Aloha	OR
Flight Coordinators	800-544-3644	310-581-5600	Santa Monica	CA P
Fly Wise Travel	800-347-3939	212-869-2223	New York	NY B
Global Adventures	800-989-6017	925-689-8883	Concord	CA P
Global Travel Con	800-366-3544	310-581-5610	Santa Monica	CA T
Group & Leisure	800-874-6608	816-690-4040	Oak Grove	MO P
GTT International	800-878-4283	972-960-2000	Dallas	TX T
Hostways Travel	800-327-3207	954-966-8500	Ft. Lauderdale	FL B
HTI Tours	800-441-4411	215-563-8484	Philadelphia	PA T
Intair Transit		514-286-7078	Montreal	PQ T
Integrity Travel	800-468-4272	406-755-8484	Kalispell	MT P
J & O Air	800-877-8111	619-282-4124	San Diego	CA T
Jaya Travel	877-359-5292	312-606-9600	Chicago	IL P
		248-372-4800	Southfield	MI
		212-697-0022	New York	NY
Jensen Baron	800-333-2060	801-267-5757	Salt Lake City	UT B
Jetset Tours Inc.	800-638-3273	323-290-5800	Los Angeles	CA T
King Tut Tours, Inc.	800-398-1888	510-791-2907	Fremont	CA B
McAbee Tours	800-622-2335	770-396-9988	Atlanta	GA T
Midtown Tvl Cons	800-548-8904	404-872-8308	Atlanta	GA B
Mill-Run Tours	800-645-5786		Miami	FL T
		312-641-5914	Chicago	IL
		201-894-1200	Englew'd Cliffs	NJ
		212-486-9840	New York	NY
		713-961-3666	Houston	TX
Moment's Notice		212-486-0500	New York	NY P
Mr. Cheap's		212-431-1616	New York	NY P

Odyssey Travel		613-549-3553	Kingston	ON P
		613-789-1900	Ottawa	ON
Pacific Gateway	800-777-8369	503-294-6478	Portland	OR T
	800-777-8369	206-624-2228	Seattle	WA
Pali Tours & Travel		808-533-3608	Honolulu	HI B
Panda Travel	800-447-2632	602-943-3383	Phoenix	AZ P
Pennsylvania Tvl	800-331-0947	610-251-9944	Paoli	PA P
Picasso Travel	800-742-2776	310-645-4400	Los Angeles	CA T
Raptim Travel	800-777-9232	716-754-9232	Lewiston	NY B
Regatta Travel	800-445-7685	303-751-0666	Aurora	CO P
Reko Tours	800-536-1866	718-932-3232	Astoria	NY T
Riverside Travel		808-521-5645	Honolulu	HI P
Royal Lane Travel	800-329-2030	214-340-2030	Dallas	TX B
RTS Travel Svcs	800-853-1128	850-243-2662	Ft. Walton Bch	FL P
Rupa Travel Svc		732-572-5000	Edison	NJ B
Seamorgh Travel	800-543-2994	973-376-1141	Millburn	NJ B
Sharp Travel	800-220-2165	301-731-3355	Landover	MD B
Sky Bird Travel	887-759-2473	312-606-9600	Chicago	IL T
		248-372-4800	Southfield	MI
		212-697-0022	New York	NY
STA Travel	800-781-4040			P
	800-777-0112	(nat'l res. ctr.)	Scottsdale	AZ
		602-921-1988	Tempe	AZ
		510-642-3000	Berkeley	CA
		323-934-8722	Los Angeles	CA
		310-824-1574	Los Angeles	CA
	800-925-4777	(groups)	Los Angeles	CA
		619-270-1750	San Diego	CA
		415-391-8407	San Francisco	CA
		310-394-5126	Santa Monica	CA
		202-877-0912	Washington	DC
		202-887-7800	Washington	DC
		305-284-1044	Coral Gables	FL
		352-338-0068	Gainesville	FL
		407-541-2000	Orlando	FL
		813-974-3380	Tampa	FL
		312-786-9050	Chicago	IL
		504-334-2516	Baton Rouge	LA
		617-373-7900	Boston	MA
		617-266-6014	Boston	MA
		617-576-4623	Cambridge	MA

STA Travel		734-968-5151	Ann Arbor	MI	P
(cont'd)		612-615-1800	Minneapolis	MN	
		212-627-3111	New York	NY	
		212-865-2700	New York	NY	
		215-568-7999	Philadelphia	PA	
		215-382-2928	Philadelphia	PA	
		512-472-2900	Austin	TX	
		804-924-4445	Charlottesville	VA	
		206-633-5000	Seattle	WA	
		608-263-8810	Madison	WI	
Sun Destination		415-398-1313	San Francisco	CA	P
Sunny Land Tours	800-783-7839	201-487-2150	Hackensack	NJ	B
Supersonic Travel		323-851-0333	Hollywood	CA	B
TFI Tours Int'l	800-745-8000	212-736-1140	New York	NY	B
The Last Min Club	800-563-2582	416-441-2582	North York	ON	P
Ticket Planet	800-799-8888	415-288-9999	San Francisco	CA	B
Trade Wind Assoc	800-268-4853	604-683-6900	Vancouver	BC	B
	800-438-4853	312-664-3434	Chicago	IL	
	800-438-4853	212-286-0667	New York	NY	
	800-268-4853	416-966-4853	Toronto	ON	
	800-438-4853	713-960-0343	Houston	TX	
Trans Am Travel	800-600-1567	310-670-2111	Los Angeles	CA	T
		415-397-1122	San Francisco	CA	
	800-822-7600	312-214-4411	Chicago	IL	
	800-822-7600	212-730-4980	New York	NY	
	800-600-1548	703-998-7676	Alexandria	VA	
	800-553-6762	703-912-3900	Burke	VA	B
Travac Tours	800-872-8800	407-896-0014	Orlando	FL	B
Travel Avenue	800-333-3335	312-876-6866	Chicago	IL	P
Travel Center, Inc.	800-621-5228	312-726-0088	Chicago	IL	B
Travel Desk	800-328-5377	612-835-9697	Bloomington	MN	B
Travel Express	800-333-3611	801-483-6120	Salt Lake City	UT	T
Tvl Leaders Int'l	800-323-3218	305-443-7755	Coral Gables	FL	T
Travel 'N Tours	800-984-9075	914-838-2600	Beacon	NY	B
Travel Network		423-485-1291	Chattanooga	TN	P
Travel Network	800-929-1290	540-891-2929	Fredericksburg	VA	P
Travel Team	800-788-0829	206-301-0443	Seattle	WA	P
Travelink	800-525-2560	303-792-3124	Englewood	CO	T
Tulips Travel	800-882-3383	212-490-3388	New York	NY	B

Uniglobe Amer		504-561-8100	New Orleans	LA	B
Unitravel	800-325-2222	314-569-0900	St. Louis	MO	B
Value Holidays	800-558-6850	414-241-6373	Mequon	WI	B
WalkerHill W'wide	800-568-2835	212-221-1234	New York	NY	B
Worldwide Travel	800-343-0038	202-659-6430	Washington	DC	B
	800-820-8440	703-820-9700	Alexandria	VA	
Zig Zag Travel	800-726-0249	718-575-3434	Rego Park	NY	B

Chapter Six

Consolidators Around the World

Consolidators are not a purely American phenomenon. In fact, the need for a parallel grey market in airlines tickets is felt more keenly in other parts of the world where national airlines set their tariffs unreasonably high and stick to the rules of the IATA price-fixing cartel. So it's not surprising that in some more freewheeling cities around the world consolidators abound.

Most of these operations are what are known as "bucket shops." It's a term that seems to have originated in England, along London's King's Road, which became a district known for its budget travel agencies catering to long-range, long-term, back-packing travelers. "Bucket shop" was originally a derogatory term but it seems to have lost its negative connotations.

Bucket shops are discount travel agencies, as opposed to wholesalers. They are able to sell tickets cheaply by using a number of legal ploys that allow them to subvert the price-fixing rules set down by IATA, the International Air Transport Association, which state that no member airline may sell below tariff. These ploys include rebated commissions and bulk sales of tickets. The precise strategy the bucket shop uses is of less interest than its ability to get you a cheap ticket. Rest assured that when you deal with a bucket shop, you are not dealing with some shady operator or breaking any local ordinances.

There is nothing to stop you from dealing with a consolidator in another country, either by a long-distance phone call before you leave home, or in person once you arrive. International phone rates are dropping rapidly so it can be very cheap to pick up the phone and call overseas.

A foreign consolidator can help you extend your reach and stretch your travel dollar by providing you with a cheap ticket to a still more exotic destination. For example, you might fly to London and then join the hordes of British holidaygoers boarding cheap flights to Cyprus. Or jet to Bangkok and pick up a cheap flight to India. Don't automatically assume, however, that this will be the cheapest way to reach your ultimate destination. Check with the stateside consolidators listed earlier to get a basis for comparison. And a good around-the-world specialist should be plugged in to sources of good deals throughout the world.

It might be argued that splitting your trip with two consolidator tickets, one bought here and one overseas, allows you a free stopover in the overseas consolidator's city, but a good domestic around-the-world specialist can arrange free stopovers en route. So check first. Still, it's possible that a foreign bucket shop may have access to deals your local consolidator knows nothing about.

The best times to use a foreign bucket shop are:

- When you are flying on a frequent flyer award that can't get you where you really want to go. In this case your trip to the foreign city is "free."
- When you're stuck. If you suddenly find you need a one-way ticket home, seek out a bucket shop.
- On the spur of the moment. Not every trip is preplanned down to the last minute. If you find Hong Kong getting boring, why not hop on a cheap flight to Kathmandu!

With a bit of luck, you should be able to find a source of cheap tickets just about anywhere, but really good consolidators are found in just a handful of international cities where market conditions allow them to flourish The contacts listed in this chapter have been gleaned from a variety of sources and reflect the bucket shop "hot spots" around the world.

We split the listings below into Europe and Asia and then

subdivide by city, in alphabetical order. We list the consolidator's name, local phone number, and web site(if available).

Note that to dial the local numbers from abroad, you must include the appropriate access and country codes and drop the initial zero in the local listing. Check your local phone directory for access and country codes.

Europe

Amsterdam	European Travel Network	020-622-6473
Amsterdam	Future Line Travel	020-622-2859
Amsterdam	NBBS Reizen	020-626-2557
Amsterdam	Near East Tours	020-646-4747
Amsterdam	Nouvelles Frontieres	020-664-0447
Athens	Intertrust Travel	01-3234910
Berlin	Air Travel Service (ATS) www.ats.de	049-30-896-996-0
Bonn	Reisen Ticketman www.travelcenter.de	0228-96-45-00
Bonn	Teletravel www.tele-travel.de	0228-26-70-20
Dusseldorf	Trans-Tasya Reisen www.transtasya.de	049-211-47126-0
Frankfurt	Flugmarkt	069-690-307-21
Frankfurt	Last Minute Reiseburo	069-96740-099
Frankfurt	STA Travel www.sta-travel.com	069-97907-456
Haarlem	Montys Travel Service www.montys.nl	023-532-8255
Hamburg	TopTravel www.toptravel.de	040-389-1000
Heilbronn (Ger)	Take Off Reisen www.take-off-reisen.de	071-312591-0
London	Air Travel Advisory Bureau	0171-251-2277
London	Alpha Flights	0171-609-8188
London	American Travel	0171-722-0202
London	Bridge The World www.b-t-w.co.uk	0171-734-7447

London	Campus Travel	0171-730-3402
London	Charter Flight Centre	0171-828-1090
London	Classic Travel	0171-499-2222
London	Columbus Direct www.columbusdirect.co.uk	0171-375-0011
London	Condor Travel	0171-373-0495
London	Council Travel www.counciltravel.com	0171-287-3337 (Europe) 0171-437-7767 (W'wide)
London	East To West Travel	0171-240-4050
London	Eurotours www.eurotours.co.uk	0181-289-8889
London	Farnley Travel	0171-930-7679
London	Fine Quote	0171-240-4400
London	FlightBookers www.flightbookers.com	0171-757-2000
London	Galaxy Travel	0181-925-0055
London	German Travel Centre	0181-429-2900
London	Globe Savers	0875-556-556
London	Golden Sands Travel	0181-297-9987
London	Interjet Holidays	0181-882-8882
London	Just The Ticket www.justtheticket.co.uk	0171-291-8111
London	Nouvelles Frontieres	0171-620-1100
London	Shortbreaks	0181-402-0007
London	STA Travel www.sta-travel.com	0171-581-4132
London	The Flight Centre	0181-858-6677
London	The Travel Bug www.travel-bug.co.uk	0171-835-2000
London	Trailfinders	0171-938-3366 0171-937-5400
London	Travel Arcade	0171-734-5873
London	Travel Zone	0171-287-8997
London	TravelSavers www.comettravel.demon.co.uk	0171-437-7878
London	US Airtours www.usairtours.co.uk	0990-28-0003

London	USIT Campus www.usitcampus.co.uk	0870-240-1010
Munich	Council Travel www.counciltravel.com	089-39-50-22
Munich	Flugborse www.fly.de	01805-252555
Munich	Travel Overland www.travel-overland.de	089-27276-300
Paris	Council Travel www.counciltravel.com	01-44-41-89-89
Paris	ITS International	01-42-25-92-90
Paris	Compagnie des Voyages www.lcdv.com	01-45-08-44-88
Prague	Action Travel	2242-32474
Prague	Tom's Travel www.travel.cz	2331-339-666

Asia & Australia

Auckland	STA Travel www.sta-travel.com	09-309-0458
Bangkok	Airland	02-255-5432
Bangkok	Airspan Network	02-718-7041
Bangkok	Chawla Travel www.chawlatravel.com	02-237-0990
Bangkok	Compass Travel www.compasstravel-thailand.com	02-652-0714
Bangkok	Dits Travel www.diethelm-travel.com	02-255-9205-15
Bangkok	DTC Travel Company www.dtctravel.com	02-259-4535
Bangkok	Pawana Tour & Travel www.pawanatour.com	02-267-8018
Bangkok	Skyline Travel Services	02-260-5525
Bangkok	STA Travel www.sta-travel.com	02-236-0262
Hong Kong	Aero International Travel www.aerohkg.com	02-2543-3800
Hong Kong	Connaught Travel Ltd.	02-2544-1531

Hong Kong	Four Seasons Travel	02-2868-0622
Hong Kong	Marvel Tours Ltd.	02-2722-1001
Hong Kong	Rocksun Travel Agency	02-2869-6838
Hong Kong	Skyway Travel	02-2781-1823
Hong Kong	Travel Expert	02-2845-3232
Kuala Lumpur	STA Travel www.sta-travel.com	03-248-9800
Melbourne	STA Travel www.sta-travel.com	03-9876-8211
Nagoya	No. 1 Travel	052-243-1681
Osaka	GS Travel	06-6281-1230
Singapore	CIEE Travel	734-0001
Singapore	STA Travel www.sta-travel.com	737-7188
Sydney	Cyber Air Broker www.airdiscounter.com	02-9232-5677
Sydney	Skylink Travel www.skylink.com.au	02-9223-4277
Sydney	STA Travel www.sta-travel.com	02-9314-7888
Sydney	Travel.com.au www.travel.com.au	02-9249-5444
Tokyo	A'cross Travellers Bureau	03-5467-0077
Tokyo	Beltop Travel Service www.beltop.com	03-3211-6555
Tokyo	Cheetah Tour	03-5403-2538
Tokyo	Council Travel www.counciltravel.com	03-5467-5535
Tokyo	Flex International www.flex-inter.co.jp/english.html	03-3233-8861
Tokyo	Hit Travel www.findex.ne.jp/hit/	03-3473-9040
Tokyo	No. 1 Travel	03-3200-8871
Tokyo	STA Travel www.sta-travel.com	03-5485-8380
Tokyo	Travel Hero Corp. www.travel-hero.co.jp	03-3555-5888

**Visit The Intrepid Traveler
on the Internet
http://www.intrepidtraveler.com**

**Saving you a fortune...
one trip at a time**

More Resources for the Intrepid Traveler
Expand Your Budget Travel Horizons

Air Courier Bargains —
How To Travel World-Wide For Next To Nothing (Seventh Edition)
Kelly Monaghan $14.95   ©1999   224 pages
Want to fly from New York to Paris for $199, round-trip? Or from Miami to Madrid for $99. Or from L.A. to Bangkok for free? Sound impossible? It's not! Every day, hundreds of people take off to exotic ports of call as air couriers. Those sitting next to them on the plane have no idea of their "secret mission." They certainly don't know that the courier beside them paid only a fraction of the lowest available fare. In fact, the courier might even be flying **for free!**

An air courier is someone who accompanies time-sensitive cargo shipped as passengers' baggage on regularly scheduled airlines. Sometimes these people are employees of air freight companies. Most of the time, they are "freelancers," ordinary people — like you! — who perform a valuable service for the air freight company in exchange for a deep, deep discount on their roundtrip air fare.

Being an air courier requires no training, no advanced degrees, no special knowledge of the air freight business. **Anyone can be an air courier.** All it takes is a yen for low-cost travel, a taste for adventure, and the right insider contacts — contacts that *Air Courier Bargains* provides in abundance.

"An extraordinary value! The definitive book on the subject."
Arthur Frommer

Fly Cheap!
Kelly Monaghan $14.95   ©1999   256 pages
Leisure fares are up. Business fares are through the roof. The airlines want to force your travel agent out of business. And wherever you go on the Internet, you're quoted a different "lowest fare." What's a traveler to do?

Now more than ever, knowledge is power in the never-ending fight to hang on to your travel dollar. *Fly Cheap!* reveals the hidden secrets, the sneaky tricks, the insider contacts, and the plain old common sense you need to:

- Fly free! (It can still be done when you fly as an air courier.)
- Use the airlines' own rules to *your* advantage, not theirs.
- Get every discount to which you are entitled.
- Amass a treasure trove of frequent flyer miles.
- Grab huge airfare bargains overseas.
- Use the Internet wisely, not blindly.
- And much, much more.

"More unique facts about how to get deals that save you money than I've ever seen in one book."
John Clayton, KKGO-FM, Los Angeles

Become a Home-Based Travel Agent and buy consolidator tickets at low, low agents-only fares

Home-Based Travel Agent —
How To Cash In On The Exciting NEW World Of Travel Marketing
Kelly Monaghan $29.95   ©1997, 1999   400 pages

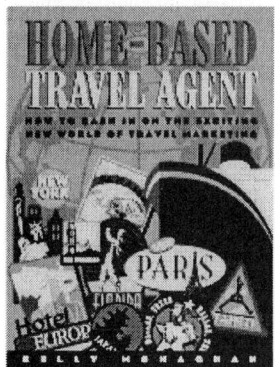

Here's your chance to join the growing number of people who are earning good money and FREE trips just by sharing their love of travel with their friends and neighbors. Recent changes in the travel marketplace have created unparalleled opportunities for you to grab a piece of the $30,000,000,000 (*thirty billion*) travel market. What once was available only to a closed shop of "travel professionals" is now open to all.

YOU can become a Home-Based Travel Agent
— *INSTANTLY* —
and start earning $50, $100, $200 (*or more*)
for every trip you book!

This book reveals the secrets you need to:
- Open your own home-based travel agency.
- Avoid high start-up costs and limit your initial investment to pocket change.
- Book air travel, tours, cruises, hotels, and car rentals like a pro — and make money every time you do.
- Gain access to the airlines' sophisticated computerized reservations systems for just $15 a month.
- Buy a $1,200 airline ticket for $800 — and then resell it for whatever the traffic will bear.
- Work part-time for pocket change or forge a full-time career.
- Take tax-deductible cruises for a fraction of their normal cost.
- Get FREE trips from tour operators eager for your business.
- Earn FREE trips just by getting as few as four people to go with you.
- Get FREE magazines and travel info to help you build your business.

This is not a once-over-lightly treatment, but a COMPLETE, easy-to-use business system. You get detailed instructions on how to set up your business, how to legally earn a commission on all travel you sell (even to yourself!), how to make your first bookings, how to find (and keep) customers, how to take advantage of the many benefits available to travel professionals, and MUCH, MUCH MORE!

Whether you just want to save some money on your own travel, start a fun part-time business out of your home, or become a six-figure, full-time travel agent, this book will tell you how. You'll save several times the cover price on the next family vacation you book using the tips contained in *Home-Based Travel Agent — How To Cash In On The Exciting NEW World Of Travel Marketing.*

"A definitive guide to getting in on the travel business. Kelly's book will tell you more than any of those mail-order deals about starting on a legitimate, part-time basis. And for lots less money."

Rudy Maxa, National Public Radio's 'Savvy Traveler'

"A gold mine of infomation for the independent contractor who wants to get his or her home-based travel business started on the right foot to success."

Gary M. Fee, Chairman, Outside Sales Support Network

"Finally, someone has written a travel agent book that tells it like it is. Kelly Monaghan's knowledge explodes off every page."

Donna M. Scherf, former Executive Director,
National Association of Commissioned Travel Agents

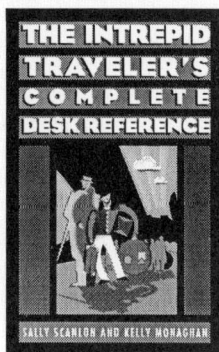

The Intrepid Traveler's Complete Desk Reference

Sally Scanlon and Kelly Monaghan

$16.95   ©1998   375 pages

What's an arunk? If you're flying into AUA, where are you going? The answers to these and thousands of other questions will be found in *The Intrepid Traveler's Complete Desk Reference*, an indispensable reference work for anyone who is really serious about travel. And if you're buying *Home-Based Travel Agent: How To Cash In On The Exciting NEW World Of Travel Marketing*, this book can help you look like a pro almost overnight! Here you'll find not just the definitions of common and obscure travel terms, but the kind of industry information a travel agent needs handy every day:

- The three-letter codes for every airport in the world, which make booking reservations a snap.
- Codes for hotels and rental cars.
- An extensive directory of toll-free numbers and web sites for suppliers — airlines, hotels, rental cars, tour operators, and cruise lines.
- Complete listings of travel organizations and publications.
- Detailed information on how to get passports and visas.
- Time zones around the world at a glance.
- The currency of every country in the world.
- Sources of FREE travel information, across the nation and around the world.
- A complete glossary of travel-related terms, acronyms, and abbreviations.

A Shopper's Guide To Independent Agent Opportunities (5th ed.)
Kelly Monaghan $49.95   ©2000

There are a growing number of outfits offering you the chance to become a travel agent — overnight — and start reaping the many benefits available to the travel industry insider. But which one is right for you?

This information-packed Special Report, containing in-depth profiles of more than 100 companies, provides you with straightforward, *unbiased* information about the current crop of offerings.

In this no-holds-barred report, you will learn . . .

- How to evaluate an outside agent opportunity.
- What the glossy brochures *don't* tell you.
- How to find the best deals.
- The hard questions to ask before signing up with any company.
- Which companies charge *no sign-up fees whatsoever.* (And which ones charge the most!)
- What you get from each company. And just as important, what you *don't* get.
- The truth about travel industry benefits and why many companies offering outside agent opportunities don't want to tell you about it.

Get past the hype and the salesmanship. Get the straight information from someone who's been there. This insider information — not available anywhere else — will save you weeks of research time and let you narrow your search for an outside agent relationship that will work for you. It can also save you thousands of dollars in sign-up charges and annual fees.

**YOU CAN'T GET THIS INSIDE INFORMATION
ANYWHERE ELSE!**

YOUR TICKET TO SAVING *BIG* MONEY ON TRAVEL

☐	*YES!* I want to succeed in my own home-based travel marketing business! Send me the Complete Home-Based Travel Agent System for just $69.95. (<u>Counts as 3 books when figuring shipping</u>.) I prefer to order separately:

☐ *Home-Based Travel Agent: How To Cash In On*
The Exciting NEW World of Travel Marketing $29.95

☐ *The Intrepid Traveler's Complete Desk Reference* $16.95

☐ *A Shopper's Guide To Independent Agent Opportunities* $49.95

☐ I need another copy of *Air Travel's Bargain Basement*, for just $9.95

☐ I want to travel the world as an air courier. Send me *Air Courier Bargains* for just $14.95.

☐ I want to beat the airlines at their own game. Send me *Fly Cheap!* for just $14.95

Delivery Options: For regular postage (Special 4th Class Book Rate), add $3.50 for the 1st book and $.50 for each additional book ordered. Allow 3 to 4 weeks for delivery. For faster UPS delivery, add to the book total $5.00 for the 1st book and $1.00 for each additional book ordered. For foreign delivery (except Canada), add 15% to "Total" for surface mail; for air mail costs email us at info@intrepidtraveler.com or fax 212-942-6687. **U.S. funds only.**	Book total	
	NY tax (8.25%)*	
	Regular postage	
	or UPS delivery	
	TOTAL	

*NY residents only

Name: _____

Address: _____
<small>UPS can deliver only to street addresses (no P.O. boxes) in the continental US.</small>

City: _____ State: _____ Zip: _____

Visa/MC/Amex: _____ Exp.: _____

Signature _____ Phone: _____

E-mail (for regular updates) _____

Make checks payable to:

The Intrepid Traveler • Box 438 • New York, NY 10034-0438
Fax credit card orders to 212-942-6687
Prices & availability subject to change without notice.

For more great books and tons of travel info visit our web site
http://www.intrepidtraveler.com

ATB